In Memory of Her

Rosemarie Rowley

Rowan Tree Press

ISBN 978 1 872224 03 2
Printed by Naas Printing Ltd., Naas, Co. Kildare

Also by Rosemarie Rowley:

Poetry

The Broken Pledge	Martello, Dublin, 1985
The Sea of Affliction	
a work of eco-feminism	Comark, Rowan Tree Press, 1987
Flight into Reality	Rowan Tree Press, 1989
Politry	Rowan Tree Press 1988
Hot Cinquefoil Star	Rowan Tree Press, 2002 inc. *Flight into Reality, The Poet's Visit, The Puzzle Factory, A Ruby Garland for George and Nora, Letter to Kathleen Raine*

Translations:
You Are the Earth from the Italian of Mimmo Morina,
Alma Tellus from the Italian of Mimmo Morina,
Euro Editions, 1996 1997.

Anthologies:
Extended Wings, 1993, 1994 (editor),*Seeing the Wood and the Trees* editor with John Haughton, Forest Friends Ireland with Rowan Tree Press, 2003
The Book of Cabra (ed. Dermot Bolger) *Poets for Africa* (ed. Lynda Moran) *Byzantium* (ed. Gearailt Mac Eoin)
Voices from Wollaston Lake (eds. Goldstick and Graham)
And God Created Woman (ed. Susan White) *Between Innocence and Peace* (ed. Brendan Kennelly) *Galway's Pirate Women* (ed. Margretta D'Arcy) *Extended Wings* (ed. Christine Broe) *An Bhileog Bhan – The White Page* (ed. Joan McBreen),*Image* Maxwell House short story award, 1988 ..*"there was a house"*
Anonymous Women Bards of Connaught – Thessaloniki European Capital of Culture, 1997; BBC Woman's Hour, May 1998.

Author's Note

This book is dedicated to all those women whose lives, living or dead, continue to inspire, fascinate, or terrify me.

And to those men whose encouragement enabled me to become a better person, mother, and creative artist – especially my late father, George Rowley, traditional musician.

I would like to express my heartfelt thanks to my brother Joe, and his wife Mary, and my whole family whose support has been crucial over the years.

A special thanks to my Leitrim kinswomen, Margaret Burns, Mairead Flynn, Mary Guckian and Anne Muldowney, and Berna Egar, a kinswoman from Cork, who were always available when I needed to discuss some difficult questions and whose inspiration and practical help were given unstintingly.

And I would be nowhere at all without my wonderful son David, whose love and patience at all times enabled me to carry on with my work.

Acknowledgements are due to the editors of

*New Writing- Books Ireland; Dun Laoghaire-Rathdown
Arts Publications*; *Electric Acorn; Extended Wings; The
Irish Times; The Irish Press*; *Nouvel Europa; Reddest
Stolen Cherries; Riposte; Voices from Wollaston Lake*;
and *Womanspirit,* in which these poems, or versions of
them, first appeared.

The author would like to acknowledge assistance from
An Chomhairle Ealaion - The Arts Council, Dublin, for
providing several grants enabling her to travel to literary
events abroad.

Thanks are due to Henry Mair and Sam Gilliland for
their Trojan work in organizing and judging the Scottish
Open International Poetry Competition for the past 40
years.

And to Philip Casey, for assistance in going on-line.

Cover illustration and design by Rosemarie Rowley

Website: www.rosemarierowley.ie

Contents

POEMS WRITTEN ON CERTAIN OCCASIONS

Epic Award Winners

Selected Earlier Poems

From *The Broken Pledge*

From *The Sea of Affliction*

BROKEN FLOWERS
i.m. Ann, my sister 1947 – 1997)

Heads of fine purple strewn across cement
And yellowness heaped up in an airless room –
Travesties to which your heart's golden fire-dust
Is an increment on pain. You asked
If the pretence of caring had now vanished,
Was it real now, under the cracked sky-line,
Like your memories dammed up under the rain.

Surely some vital drops will float
To pull your rootless beauties into holiness
Even as they die in a still vase –
There is no picture to quite stir the heart
As these fallen crowns, noble as the chalice
Of Gethsemane, which yet held the terrifying
Dark secrets of the world's crime.

As you winter in your youth,
Beheaded flowers your beauty, your truth.

NO TEA PARTY

The lid is rising on the kettle's song,
Likewise my energy wastes itself in air,
Don't call me when the tea's made, I'll be gone.

I left my true self with your vulgar throng
Now drawn and quartered, they arraign me with a stare,
The lid is rising on the kettle's song.

To have believed in you, and not in long
Speeches of your drab affair –
Don't call me when the tea's made, I'll be gone.

No one pushed me, but I see that I was wrong,
I've said it all, but I won't bow, so there!
The lid is rising on the kettle's song.

I should have known it, and the bells can bong
Each Sunday of the year without our heir,
Don't call me for the christening, I'll be gone

I did without a wedding, honeymoon, even the pong
Of babies, so there's no joy for us to share –
The lid is hopping on the kettle's song –
Don't call me. When the tea's made, I'll be gone.

A WREATH FOR SAINT VALENTINE'S DAY

A clew within this virgin card from the head
Which you denied and now which gives you hope
Has come to me. When you opened your mouth
The scent of honeysuckle drenched my shoulder
Your hair tossed, though neatly cut
Still betraying my wild, rapturous caress
Your eyes, that were soft, are now sharp -
Knowing pollution, spoilage, missiles;
Behaving with me with speech-robbing words,
Soul-hurting cynicism, lethal logic.

Now I'm staked to the ground, a paling
Around my house where golden children
Will never flower, who once flowered
In your heart of satin's reddest hearts.

MUST I CALL YOU.....AGAIN?

Must I call you again, onlooker at my hurt,
Talking by the window, an inscape of wrecked
Solitude, impugned bad manners, and the curt
Commerce of refusal. Your blameless, decked

Hand of fate. Capitulation, a trade or pain
Of being alone. What mannered smile can lift
My woebegone future for the pull of rain
Making the shards of bright light shift

Away from wonderment, green-begetting magic?
An empowerment of the seeing eye inwards,
Making whole my patchwork, your solipsism so tragic,
In a smitten whorl of entire fate dragged skin-wards,

Renting with ache this sojourning material,
Glimpsing the light eternal, ethereal.

THE DISTRACTED SCHOLAR

Across the page in gothic script
Your clever hand has made a word
It gently sits upon my ripped
Peace like a singing bird

The word is proof you're in the world -
I touch the page, it whispers faintly
With your voice, when the questions hurled
Against what you said was stone quaintly

Dead, when life itself was resurrection -
Or rather: *You are at the edge of my dream*
Waving to me like a mood – like the confection
Of deeds I uttered as if the lip of seem

Were nothing. Why trouble you with this?
   -    you have written on the page your kiss.

THE UNREPENTANT VIRAGO

Named for a man, my treason's not my own
My tantalising tales tame his temerity
As I cling to the cliff-hanger
Of my own biopic, my to-be-tested verity
He claims I am inevitable as the ocean
And my head will roll, be beached upon the sand
And he will come and take me by the hand.

I will scream loudly history's muffling cry
Show female slavery, oppression till he wonders why
The goddess in him was quenched, and died of thirst
He thinks then that I will be the first
To bandage up his Achilles heel with Elastoplast!

Published, I' m not damned, but live with gumption
I'm here to fix his arrogant presumption.

LUST IS AS ILL-CONSIDERED A WEED
AS EVER STOLE SCENT

Rejected in the main as superstition -
A gadfly, I'm alone upon the weed:
A hot cinquefoil brooding on position,
Declared intent of being in need of screed -

Now the subject of each idle bee
Gorged already, needing a restful stop
What if his gyrations bring to me
No true syncopation of a honeyed hop?

Beauty – not recognised as such – I wonder
Why man and woman excavate a flower garden
Tear my fertility, so they may squander
Wild possibility, and the earth around me harden.

Can the joy I have before I'm torn asunder
Be worth it when they never ask my pardon?

JADE

I knew you fainthearted what side you were on
When you talked of social reality: not Jesus at the well
With the Samaritan woman, or the invisible loss of
power
Which halts her speech and causes His deference

Holding her in trust for what she is.
You can talk of rural communes in China
Till the cows come home – leading them will be a girl
Bearing a key-ring and a dead black raven.

Your ways are sweet indeed, nectar and honey
And vinegar to end it all: you'd let all the
Wells in the world run dry for a principle
And proudly show us the papier-mache women who
survived,

Embalmed with bitter hope and urgent salvation,
To tell the tale on electro-magnetic tape.

WOMAN WRITER

If interviewed on the subject of the sonnet
What man has brought me endless cups of tea?
They'll say I've got a Queen Bee in my bonnet
The male groupies will not type my poems for me.

What golden mother lives without inspiration?
What sister can be truly herself, and tackle
The canon in the patriarchal cold, the purgation
Of miles of libraries with the truth a hackle?

The worst thing is that there's no male muse -
I don't feel the marginalisation or the neglect
Quite as much as the possibility I might lose
The reader in the absence of his call-collect -

And I must be very careful with my man -
I lose a husband if I kiss a fan.

ON HIS BIRTHDAY

from Anne Donne to her husband John – supposing she went on record..

Five senses have we, but just one soul
I take you part by part, and then the whole
Your fingertips begin at shadow's end
And I on each a hundred kisses spend.

Your toes from which radiate your joy
Your soles, your feet, your legs I all enjoy
Your shoulders, arms, are ceaseless comfort trained
Your face, your hair, your lips are thus arraigned.

Sweet tower of enterprise, and honeyed substance found
We share our treasure where we most abound
Our secret selves are now a flame of sense
Where we explode at last in innocence.

Exploring ways to end all life's regrets
Our joy a million, million tears forgets.

THE MOON HANKERS

Though none can comfort me, nor sage, nor oak
Nor heart of bronze made in a silver hoop
With gem encrusted golden rod to poke
Out my eyes in mystery's final scoop -

Flanged with crimson, dreaming the polite
And suave boulvardiers of a nation
To feel myself what precious little light
Man's first step has had upon my station -

I'd seek you out, you sapphire of the seam
Until you'd say I'd swallow back the sea -
How like a comfortless queen I'd deem
Myself as such heaven bent to me,

Leaving me lonely in the western sky
Beckoning you hither for eternity.

ALMOST AN APOLOGY

Sometimes he enchants me with his word
The sea of phrases laps around my feet
His vision hones on truth just as a bird
Seeks its mate to fit a fancy, greet

With the sun each rising lovely day
Preens his feathers shining in the wood
As a flowered clearing on the first of May
Seeks redemption for all Adam's brood -

The twain, the pair, the loser man with Eve
Stumbling on knowledge – a foxglove's draught
A sweet sip to stage a sin, as if to grieve
Hard labour, the smithy's spear and shaft

To gauge surrender, 'twixt good and evil torn -
To gouge the heart, this child of woman born.

LETTER TO SAPPHO

You called up the feeling. If. To brush
My import to a worldly period. Yet
As words ascend the air, finding my core lush
As Sybarites bar-tending a dream, I get
A pain in my heart that shows I'm a shadow
Pounding on the walls of my own prison.
Somewhere the music dies.. did you, Sappho,
Die of the silent centuries' excision

What poems that must sing, need to say?
Who tortured your living heart, made sever
Voice from the lingua franca, No word astray
Nor daytime deeds that make economy, never
Asking if such extinction needs YOUR autograph
For tomorrow's lot, women. Your holograph -

FOR MARY MAGDALENE

Between necessity and freedom I was crucified
Perceiving Himself endlessly on the cross
Yet aware, as an onlooker, petrified
My vision that never was, would be His loss.

I mimed too, as they hammered in the nails
Once more assuaging myself in His deep tears
Once more my heart rallying where my speech fails
To give His lips the vinegar it fears.

Sun eclipsed, I dallied with the vision of day,
A multi-chromed banner the old enemy was twisting,
Till I could no longer read in stone and clay,
My flower-head lopped, topped to the moment's listing -

I shone for Him like a speck in the glory of the sunrise
Waiting for twilight, the beauty of the stars' surprise.

THE LIFE THIEF

The Thief to Troth, the absent venery
Of heart unto dear Heart, the chase was on.
To potted meats, and murky bedchambers,
Whichever was hottest. The craft to weal,
To heal the wounded hart, the mirror anodyne
Where bishops had built enclaves in the pews,
Whose motion was the sea.
                         Your death was not news,
When, merged in the fell proof of sin
Incumbent on the age we live in
Your first cry was your last.
Not bride, but fettered in this sinning,
In your end is my beginning,
Your life, thus ended, just began another's,
Its deep bite biting, that it was your mother's.

THE PASSIONLESS REVOLUTIONARY

A ragged impulse – the scrivener's tetch
truncated our conversation on the working
class. Your brief was their craft
was their art, which liberation lost
to them: mine was an impounded version
of the waggoner's instance, the vetch
caught up in the wheel, thus anneal
the war on wills, the writer's mockery.

Justice, your fruitless wand and weal
is power to blow the thrust of the argument
over the innocent sweet scatterbrained
head of your sister. The lace-
maker's art has a hand in this, but
like fingerless gloves, makes raw vision blind.

MAKING HIM JEALOUS

Five lovers have I, nimble servants each
One comes to me in ardour where I teach

One comes in curiosity attired
And only leaves when senses all are fired

One comes in blossom with fidelity
He leaves behind a bird's nest in my tree

One comes to worship at my body's shrine
Leaves me devotion and a glass of wine

One comes to me without being capricious
Of all his charms I'm the most suspicious

Five faithful servants all do me adore
Until I am their servant, asking more –

I'm beggared but so rich in sex and sentiment
I'll tax them all for this faithful flower meant.

DEMI-MONDAINE

You belong in silhouette to the dream's theft
And weft with paid desire, look all adoring
At the man who's made your life bereft
Of actual household dreams, he says it's boring

Fresh linen, dimity and damask blue
Would be my veil, too, for daring
To ask: *did it happen to you too?*
And: *when did your sorrow go past caring?*

Don't try to leave this room without an answer
Or you'll turn back – the swathe of silk
In my eyes - you see, at heart a dancer
Each night I come home with the doorstep milk -

In the big bad world to be a cinch in style,
In the good small world to be a bright tear trickling.

THE POET MEETS THE JOURNO

All right, so I introduced you to each other,
She, *sotto voce,* with sweet piercing alter
Ego and intransigent integral and inviolate
Laws, you with your collection of newspaper
Cuttings of riots, strikes, and the dialectical
Alternative: mottled eyes and the poor man's pudding
Of truth, flavoured with salt fish loneliness.

In the dim furls of the watchman's banner
The night was just ending, so go to it -
Discern why I separately loved you.
As I make my way home by myself,
The pure gold of my honourable gesture
Will shine like an Indian summer on a child,
Be meditation for your spirit on our silent spring.

COLD WAR ARTIST

The art of such intention is fatigue
At living lies outside the scope of death,

To wear in the last blitzkrieg
A shroud meaning artist, a wreath

Of columbine in the hair, but the kitchen eyes,
Carbuncled knees betray the giver's art.

Down on the doorstep, she'll scrub your lies:
To her gift of total self she'll add a part -

Your own tongue sliced and severed on her plate
Of 20th century design – taste

The dust of pointillism, the cubist fate
Of newspaper and cello here embraced –

The emptiness filched from the master's past:
Mankind's death wishes, home to roost at last.

1964-1987

THE TEMPLE PROSTITUTE

The God came to me in the guise of a stranger
His gold body scent was of great sublimity
His arms were marble pillars, and his embrace
Melted the whole world on my belly.

He tuned me to the refinement of my own nature -
Pitched me so exquisitely I fell from heaven -
Totally vanquished, till I remembered
All there was of paradise, and the number seven.

He has the unfolding of centuries since
To worship me as a goddess divine,
But they couldn't build churches fast enough
To deny our union in the votive shrine.

The salt of humble pilgrims for my wantonness
I, who had everything but blessedness.

THE MAD SECRETARY

Hunched over the computer, I am mystical,
With mental white gloves and a karate belt -
A daylight cursor, but on my bicycle,
A word and energy transformer, a flickering Celt.

Such metaphysics I can make into sensation,
Turned into binary formulae by the boss,
My passion is for punctuation-
But the lingua franca doesn't give a toss.

I see the point. I accommodate the pause.
I rinse the cups and make the coffee sweet,
I am saving myself for this man of laws,
Of Brehon provenance, who will entreat

Me to be his love, his partner and co-genitor,
Of a life graph, where he can trust the monitor.

DEMETER AT THE CHINESE OPERA

So, I invited you to the Chinese Opera impulsively
Thinking of masks and dragons and triumphant mystery
I though it was time we threw off our coats
Of mourning, you for your daughter

Stopping one night, on the way home from a party,
So randomly, cruelly, killed by the monster
Who has slain more than all the century's wars
And my private sorrow for which there is no funeral.

I remember your straying husband also
Loved the Chinese Opera. What will happen
If we all meet between the acts?
Surely forgiveness will come like snow on the mountain

And we will live in a harmony that can never be
suppressed
In a slow majestic music that takes account of grief.

DAMSEL CAUSING DISTRESS

The knight errant sent for me, but I've gone missing
For three days now, while he's composed a ditty:
In the tide of feminism I still haven't given up kissing
Being what is termed fatalistically pretty -

But I can be the 'no' that makes for nice
When his flame burns under his boiler suit,
Then I'm decently torpid like a fish on ice
Where the guts need to go when the runts root -

A pillowing breast, my nightcap a soliloquy
To hell with his billowing sails and pregnant ships
Let him go, this guy who's got everything but me
With his big thighs, big legs, big hips -

All the things we women should shun
Save *satin, silk, squirm, sperm,* and ...sun.

BETTER HALF

for Roger and Tessa

I feel his presence as if he stood before me
My thoughts are tea-leaves only he can read
A brain scan shows I want him to adore me
While my heart shows for him my wanton need.

I trawl through the day, he could never bore me
I think of him even when I bleed
Heart of my heart, friend to never score me
Necklace of desire, bead after bead -

He knows my ways, how to love and shore me;
His speech shows me where and how to lead;
He never hurts, his will would never core me,
Or leave me hungry where I want to feed:

At times we see ourselves, strange and rude -
Clasp each other, beautiful and nude.

GANGSTER'S MOLL

The gangster's moll now exists
Beyond the proffered film season
Impeaching authorised fiction
With cries, and real tears. For

She and the boss presumably didn't care
To penetrate the mysterious body
Of God in the Universe, preferring
Hot shots, to the ultimate betrayal

Of people they grew up with, she doesn't tease
The short-circuit of big questions, just shrugs
And accepts his disappearance, like cash
Running in and out of a wallet.

Doesn't take it to heart or too hard,
But she's praying to get the kids' hands off the gun.

THE AMAZON MEETS THE GREEKS

When life was thick with possibility,
Before the written word and the weighing scales,
Your definitions held too much probity
In the rich seamless embroidery of our tales.

Our vanished mystery, which your history sealed
Up in the libraries of the planet's scar.
So what way to better wield a shield?
You men just skirt the theory of war!

Words became deeds – there were forests to lop!
Hard iron entered body and soul
I cherished my child as a cosmic tear-drop
Bound to osmosis in the ocean's roll,

And took the sword, and chopped my source and dower
Because you underestimated female power.

THERE IS NOTHING LIKE A DAME –
and there is no dame like a building society or a bank!

There may be nothing like me, but I assure you
the world would have gone to hell but for organised sex -
if boys and girls were left to nature's provenance,
a person like me would be nowhere at all.

Oh, I know how to milk attraction
and stabilise what is essentially of short duration:
if boys and girls were left to innocence
there'd be no delighting old men.

If that sounds unfair, I didn't make the rules -
all this spontaneity leaves everyone very poor,
the Church, the magistrates and the building societies
are all depending on the regulation of love.

It's the people who won't smile who bother me,
hard fitted, easy suited, do they think it's all for free?

THE TOKEN POETRY EDITOR

Sexless, unloved, this poem tycoon
Reads the heart's treasures as the brains' boon,
And riven with erudition, explores the spaces
Where uninvited couplets kill the places

With talk of probity and probability.
This mortgaged toad of honesty gives glee
To those who find in truth a rash offence
And save their daily lies in deference

To a lone columnist like herself, persuading
All that is needed is this harvest of envious raiding
To feed the bonfire of youth and exploitation –
The seducer's vocabulary of apt explanation

On why God is absent from the universe,
And can only be heard in exploding verse.

FOR SUSANNE

I came in search of skill and I found virtue
In your climb up the stairs you were neat and clear
Making no excuse for the way he hurt you
But you cling to reality with a straight and peer-

Less eye. On lined paper you have set your mark
What could you deviate from, if not from right
And knowing you is quite enough to park
Truth on the lines, the tine your birthright.

In this dark house Jews lived and hoped and dreamed
Of a land where their strangeness was a claim
To universal justice. How in the dark they teemed
Until hope ran like melted butter on the name

They must excise. Born in a country that did them wrong
You forbid yourself the luxury of song.

THE BRIDLE OF LOVE

Put on the bridle of love, or the dark places
Will inhabit your soul like a dream of plunder:
Put on the bit of desire, lest the old faces
Merge in passionate moments and betray wonder.

You pledge only with the combat of the hours
Your words fall in the silence, like coins jingling
Into the hand of the fortune-teller, who scours
Your reverie of love on your palm, tingling

Of a stranger. You are an actuary where a shadow
Turns fascination to death. Put on the bridle
Of tenderness - forgiveness, sad and low,
Can whistle with the raindrops, idle

As witnesses of profound truth. Curs
Snap at gentleness when their hunger stirs.

SHOT SILK

Your funeral mass was crowded
With people we hadn't seen for years
Coming to pay their respects, praising
You, as the front row were in tears.

I was behind a woman who moved
Restlessly in the wooden pew –
Her dress of shot silk proved
All who were there loved you.

Time was passing on each thread,
Like a blaze of life at the seam –
Taking off, finding instead,
The cool windows,
Where you are now a dream.

Many a rocket was launched in the air
That day, her colours in movement like a prayer.

THE WAY OF THE WORLD

World, if ever come again the frosty night
When jewelled dawn's head advanced too late
And summer was cut short as a blight
On love turned suddenly to hate!

Asking what goodness, you must answer
As if jealousy, the weapon of the porter
Made you fill his questionnaire for cancer
And then have you declared the morning's daughter -

Real talent can be virtuous because
A certainty is the bottom line -
Mediocrity is his rallying cause,
As if being clever, the world could turn you into swine.

Such fools are shocking, but keep the news discreet
When the queen is made a beggar in the street.

A LEAPING ACQUAINTANCE

O ask me if a friend is mine for keeping
And I will scroll down her countenance in years
To show acquaintance that's a target leaping

And I will tell you of the long nights' weeping
Into the valley of the corrupted seers
That her acquaintance was a target, leaping

As if acts of confidence were seeping
Down the drainpipe like a burst of tears,
Asking if a friend is for safe keeping,

Secrets unravelled in the glare, bleeping
With the traffic of the times that hooked my peers
Just ask me if her friendship's mine for keeping:

I say, a pox on their assiduous reaping
Their facts are gleaned where the bar sells beers
To show acquaintances like a target, leaping

On opportunity, grafting on chances, peeping
With trashy envious shades adrift in leers;
O ask me if this friend is worth the keeping,
I'll show an acquaintance missed the target, leaping.

THE SIBYL

If sometimes I have waited on your word,
Do not forget there is an empire
Out to the east, where freedom is muffled,
Where the autonomous cry, the great discovery

Of a soul to itself, is labelled treason;
Tied to the west, where freedom's pennant
Is torn and soiled like a prostitute's earnings.
Do not rebuke me, when I see well up

In your eyes, the free zone of my heart,
A ransom, perjured, sold in slavery
To patriarchy's fomenting lies.

Forgive my cowardice, as I rise to speak
I am speaking on behalf of millions.

THE POLITICALLY CORRECT POSTCARD

One picture is worth a thousand words
(And a flower is worth a whole lot more).
This was the import of the card you sent me,
Flu-eyed, runny nose and a sore

Throat. I was to dismiss, on the merit
Of sexism, the Sistine chapel decoration
Botticelli's *Primavera,* so disinherit
The mighty Logos and God's peroration -

Giving the kiss of life to a still-born cliché,
Gaybo playing his theme, with the wonderful score
In the sub-ed's office with the copy-boy's roar.
A photo-opportunity for the Amazon dee-jay,

Who rules the world with a golden rod -
Offer a handkerchief to the offended eye of God.

THE GRASS WIDOW

All this cowed earth in a blue jar, flowerless
Stands on the pine table. Clay and wood
Have broken spirit's voice, to endow
With uncalled for happiness your fleeting presence.

Truth is blunt in your eyes: you do not love me
Or what I seem to claim in you, parenthood and nation,
Lest I decipher too readily the code of your person
And trade it for the platitude of wealth

Joining you has become. You would rather
Speak of the turquoise found in a still cave
Than wear the married felicities of our age
Wafer thin as an advertisement page

Adorning the scattered newspaper. My hands
Touch your face. Nobody loves you like me.

ANCHORITE AT THE GATE OF HEAVEN

Not heeding brute reality, nor matter's bane
I kneel at the door of heaven, a suppliant,
Transcribing words of wisdom, like the rain
On wild flowers; the garden's hierophant:

Anointed, a habit on my body's beauty
I lie in the threshold of my tryst with God -
The first flight from earth being my duty
Becoming His perfect mean and golden rod,

I cool my heels in a dank, dark cell
Where half-light becomes my element
God's plenty in motes, with the music of the bell
A love feast of the penitent.

I rise on wings of thankfulness and praise,
Sing out in silence the glory of His ways.

THE LONGING

To be innocent is to be entirely unknown, even to oneself.

- Djuna Barnes

I am free at last to be silent, to lap
In the quiet of your promise of promise
Like the pear tree in the garden which feels
But does not ask, why such beauty here?

On rainy monsoon days locked in
Wanting to explore the sea and the galaxy,
The tree beseechingly asking the rain,
That I may not be gauged from your gaze,

To be by one companion remembered,
Name scratched out on the asylum walls.
As I was cancelling out ideals
I saw in the forest the tumult of life.

The remorse of a nymph once a virgin,
The stars were there, but of accidental origin.

THE 'FIFTIES WERE A SOMETIME THING

- a woman is a sometime thing

George Gershwin: *Porgy and Bess*

It is threatening to be different, alien
As the bras and stockings of dreaded womankind
Which she doesn't care to don with any grace
Whatever. Anxiously she surveys her form

Where she is going she has no idea,
In the fabled mirror she is the bride of Avon,
Her mother's sable brushes, potted rouge or shocking
Lipstick are not hers. Across the garden wall

Boys are climbing, daring agile boys,
Her neat head recalls the hurtful knuckles
- her mother's warning of too much abandon.
She sees one now, it could be herself,

Tow headed, dashing to her house, the curtains
Closing forever on the song she has for him.

MENARCHE

My aunt was a chanting woman singing beatitudes
Not blessed with children herself, but with faith.
But there were times I felt my mother, and her rage
Woman to woman, it was a different age.

When her knuckles imploded in my head
The place where my hair was torn screeched
Like nuns with satin ribbons on their hand-drawn
calendars.
Who were always jeering at women's good intentions.

My page had ink-stains, and when I won the scholarship,
The nuns stood behind me, and said "Betty Coyne takes
pains"
Their thoughts rained on my head, like blood markings
In the months where I would be sure to have visitors

Crouching around, saying what a pity
You didn't have to make an effort, it just came to you
naturally.

NEOPHYTE IN THE WRITING WARS

Her first question was - *when do you write?*
her pink triangle ear-rings pulling down
the flesh in her lobe. Her shorn down
indicated a strewn virginity lost in sight

and hearing of the press. But her daughter
now romping naked in the sun, a sibylline
echo of her mother, would not have the divine
gift and burden, for her toe was in the water.

Already an ad hoc embellishment of the female
fifth estate, a scrivener with dyed lace
silk knickers and love for her man a certain disgrace –
such quivering sensitivities would only impale

her hand at the odyssey of being a wife -
But wasn't writing preferable to life?

SYLVIA WAS AN 'A' STUDENT
and Alpha woman

The Abyss was bared, and malevolently yawning,
The deep black pit of endless loss to rile
You, and you didn't know the world was turning;

And you saw the winter trees in mourning
You weren't short-changed on their willing lack of guile
In the Apollonian myth - your soul was burning

Telling time too true, that spring was coming,
But you let the yellow sorrow of your bile
Flood the Arcadian dark your soul was scorning-

So, you died, without ever learning
That your Attic grace would give time its shining dial,
You did not know it then, but the world was turning,

The aureole of dawn crept in, to us a warning
We only have our children for a while
The Austrian angst in which your soul was burning,

The sense of happiness missing you by a mile –
In our Aphasian gloom, your words are burning
Up rivers, mountains, roads, with a killing style –
You didn't know it then, but the world was yearning.

BAG-LADY IN THE PORTRAIT GALLERY

In all my failed moments of ambitious grace,
The truth, swarth-headed, lifts its greenest shape
To madly light the curls of whitest lace
Edging your throat, and redeem the nape

Where a brown knob burnishes the bone.
Such well-bred tenants of the proudest hock
Like ancient grandees, dawn on my lone
Outride of the politic, and who can mock

The wasteland where now our dreams
Have only the patina of reality to make us sad,
Where derelicts abound in housing schemes
For the heart's homeless moments, and the bad

Lands of myth are skeletal. Public thresholds
Invest our private myths, and the flesh holds.

WOMEN CAN'T BE COMPASSIONATE

Women can't be compassionate, or their reputation's
dead
Can't comfort the lost tourist, he's the surrogate lover
As he sits on the theatre steps, wearing loud red
Checks and braces, bewildered when the play is over.

Women must be professional and never huddle
In doorways after rain, like an angel in a stupor
With life's rejects, looking for a cuddle
Sad casualities of money, or of having worn Lee
Cooper*.

Women can't be friends with male novelists, or film-
makers
Or poets, who want to define mistresses, and wives,
Leaving creativity to the movers and the shakers,
Taking dignitas and money out of women's lives.

This narrows the field to the tycoon, or the bore –
Feminists – choose death first! Webster's honest whore.

*Apologies to Lee Cooper – I couldn't resist the rhyme, in fact
their jeans are as good as anyone else's – at one time they were
very cool indeed.

GIVING THE LIE

No one is ever finally, anything
Not the genus, nor the father
Even if the songs they sell do not ring
Out anymore with the heart of their maker -

No one is finally silent, like a dumb waiter,
No one at last imperilled into prayer;
There is always a moment when now becomes later,
Thoughts sliding down the railing like a golden hair.

There is no actual promise in the nude barracks
(Which existed only to seal an impossible nightmare),
Something to mark the dread of the lost warlocks
Gone like the flame of non-existence with a blast of air.

No one is finally a liar, in the deepest calumny
Is buried a truth that only wished to be.

NOVICE IN THE CULTURAL REVOLUTION

When I showed you my first poems, you jeered
That a mere girl should try her hand at verse,
A craft to which the noblest mind aspires,
Remember your ideas were like a hearse

The funeral train of your life in history
Showing the nature and extent of man
Saying these poems were a mystery
When a pulse of a mechanical heart was your scan -

The poem a property, and I worse
Than a conquistadore, had just spent the purse
Of what was available - your curse
Tried to poison my well, and drown me.

But your auditorship was not ownership,
Any my spirit is still free.

POSTSCRIPT TO A PASSION

I was hoping you would prove me wrong -
Under the ship's sides the barnacles still cling -
I would have thought you'd never sell our song
But true to typecast, summer mothering -

You, too, proved to be full of guile
To love meant having, which ever was the worst -
In the quiet of my trust, so deep, so fragile
I live down the purple passage of remorse.

I'd sing you happy but you were buffoon
To my trammelled wanderings a parody
Set stiff in coupled rhymes to swoon
With the ecstatic rhetoric of equality -

So passion plundered, what's left is my disgrace
My jewelled head tortured in your embrace.

AND YOU, DARLING, WHOM I DID NOT GREET

Anche te, cara, che no salutai

And you, darling, whom I did not greet
But whom I will greet, finally. Courage!
I journey in order to flee another journey,
Our hearts must be high, high. As you well know.

High, yes, high our hearts. The sailors
Sing slowly, and the baggage exudes
The aroma of the Atlantic – a wild spirit
Will heal me, will heal me, you'll see!

From he, whom from earth to sky, Benedetta
I implore pardon in your name
If I do not search for the word for your pain,

If the neck free from this clasp
Breaks the circle of your arms
As with great force breaks a chain!

from the Italian of Guido Gozzano (1883-1916)

INSANE LIKE HERCULES?

A world to gain upon this poppy cock
Of abstruse romancing - he picks his sword,
Declines fiercely the rag and bauble hock
Which depends upon one exclamatory word!

He finds a changeling suckling at her breast
While she lifts her aproned sighs to Zeus,
He is unable to divert the old flock and rest
On the laurels of a peace that is a ruse,

His bright acceding to the changing star
Is nothing less than destiny uncouth
So when the violent magpie of the war
Plunders his nest of children without ruth

He favours cutlass ways with men,
Amputating limbs, and spilling blood again.

BEAUTY'S HELICON

I've had practice with sleeping with those who do not
please me,
I've had oceans of despair in my cup of pain,
I do not try to please those who do not please me,
They cause storms, and trigger fissures in the brain,

So when I know my true love by his hand,
I'll set in stone my long list of his beauty,
Release into the air the demons of that band
Who say the ugly are forgetful of their duty,

To live a life of honour, but not lust,
To be the clerk of passion, and its ways,
To write the bibliographies in dust,
To caption beauty in the prison of their days,

As my true love and I practice the ration
Of beauty, that makes his fidelity a passion.

GOODNESS AS A VIBRATION

I love only what is good, and this aesthetic
Delights the blind man, for he can feel
Shimmer like a moth at his elbow, my pathetic
Sighs of creation in making what's real,

And he can distinguish the dark shrouds
Of faces where wicked deeds were splendour,
He can detect the feast of envy, and loud
Avenues of fame, their soul's provender.

A child glistens with beauty like a rain-
Drop, dancing with the feet of time,
Innocence is bliss only when his pain
Of not seeing is absent, for he hurts like lime

Thrown in the faces of perceived sinners -
Who say horses backed on principle are not winners.

THE BUTTON-BACK NURTURERS

…. debt-ridden emotions and emotion-ridden debts –

Oscar Wilde on the Irish

Mothers and matriarchs, you toy the gutted room
Where sensibility is decaffeinated lace
Tireless in your role of martyr and your zoom
Lens to condemnation before an act takes place,

Your constant servitude serving only gloom
Creating recognition of what we all must face,
Death itself, never exhausted, a loom
On which your tapestry is woven, mace

Broken with your unbroken shadow. Love's vroom
Never gets off the ground or into the race
And is absent save for endless debt, a womb
Of ever-diminishing returns, and the plain case

That you can't own others, is yours alone to ponder,
In your violated abyss with its pain and rage and wonder.

MOTHER'S LITTLE KILLERS

She hates them, the unguent power
Which sticks her fairy wings together
Making impossible the ivory tower
Of disinterested passion, the if and whether

Of generic names, the ultimate aloneness.
The honest answer is to unstick
The loathsome epithets accompanying the mess
Let her soul free with a lexographic brick

As she goes on her desert train to limbo -
Grant her freedom to ride into the dusk
Without turning her into a soulless bimbo,
Pills shedding the epigrammatic husk,

Cavorting in the lunar satellite,
A spaced monkey too drugged to fight.

TRENCHANT WENCH FROM THE UNROMANTIC MIDLANDS

In the pub, I serve out the pints
My comely bosom gives a hint of home
And what men are escaping from – dreary sex
With housewives who scour the sink with vigour

Trim the joint and lard the fowl
Gristles of fat clinging to their knuckles
As the froth of beer clings to men's beards.
England is a riff between the breakfast table and tea

Where homely condiments drown the flavour
Of each day, and newspapers live on scandal
The seamier the better. It makes the ordinary man
Happier than ever not to be one of the toffs

Glad that she can be had for a song
Save the one that lies buried in her throat.

THE RELUCTANT GUEST

Not proof against the pricks disdained
By the broad impact of petty phil-
Osophy, but sundered when our passions rained
Over our heads, when wish invaded will,

I am part neighbour in this shire of doubt,
That keeps me tenant on the promised crowd
Which you waggishly say will never rout
The insane longing to impact with loud

Music the harmony of sense. Yet I fear
The submerged faculty of my wavering power
Is grief to you, a crutch for every tear,
That springs between us, to endower

Your raving optimist's cry that you're a help,
To such as me, a miserable poor whelp.

THE B.T.N. LOVE

If I had faced then the lonely hall,
The black entrance into my own absence
If I had not lifted the phone to call
Each acquaintance, would I be so tense

But my urge to love and live is so immense
These cradling arms of plastic only stale
And I am ridiculous and intense
And all rejection like a ragman's bale

With waves of pain beating on the wall
Crying to someone, somewhere, to speak sense -
My questionable right to love you all
Somehow in absence, seems that more intense,

Yet can be measured in this dying squall,
As I am waiting for your questioning call.

AUTHENTIC

There should be a doorway to love -
Some scabbard-hungry sabre to declare
What is not mine, is yours
Bawling infant of the bawdy air,
Trinketing loneliness into the poor's
Ardent threshold set with jewels rare -
Beryl and ruby; a diamond lures
Only the owner and not the loved pair.

Be one with the child of my cures
You are, you are the authentic heir.
Be with me, child of the midnight hours,
Be thou my confession in the mode of care.
Love me to death, my own creative power,
Be my own child, beyond compare.

LAMB AMONG THE LITERARY LIONS

Housewives, secretaries, the odd pro willing to stoop,
All came, delinquents, child prodigies, derelict old men
"All welcome" – the Chair of the Writers' Group
To those looking for support, with a love of the pen;

They were decent people bonding, scorning the pub
The roll call a hedge school of ancient fame
They read poems and stories like a literary club
And enjoyed playing the great writing game.

Anthology reviewed, the twelve year old took accolade
From the shyest to the most arrogant, all were shook
He was savaged by the *grande dame* in an envious raid
She was terrified someone so young would produce a
book!

Even the Chair demurred, and went to *The Times*
Requesting deletion of "all welcome "– young souls are
stilled by such crimes.

CHILD AT THE BOTANIC GARDENS

To make a phrase numismatic, it was
A day of days. My darling ran
Under the boughs of covert loss
Until God made his presence scan,

Like a metre of bright wave, the sin
Of our hearts, and I could count each blotch
Of love as I gazed upward through the din
In my breath hiding from His scotch -

But He had kind words rain on me
And the sun came out and healed the welts and hurt
Till my sadness slipped down the vast tree-
Trunks, and fell like stockings on the dirt

And slaps of time, and grubby days when He
Was absent. My son says He lives in every tree.

A CENOTAPH WOULD SPEAK OUT LOUD

There is, in my still heart, room for you,
Despite the unmannerly way you have behaved
I have managed to conserve a bloom or two.

You smiled, and said love was for the few,
The deed is done, your garden, it is paved,
In my torn heart, there's still room for you.

You said the years would bring regret and rue
As into each decade I danced and raved
I have managed to conserve a bloom or two.

I think, how, in spite of things, you're true
How, in a small place, all the people braved,
In my dying heart there's room for you.

In your slow glance, trust was built anew
Creeping home, someone smiled at me and waved,
I have managed to conserve a bloom or two.

In your name, I watch the stars turn blue,
Is there a chance somehow I'll be saved?
In my eternal heart, there's a bloom or two,
I have managed to save a room for you.

WORLD WAR THREE BLUES

I shall not pay a zloty for a Zeppelin
The dirigible balloon that croons to consort with air
Better than bands-trot bunting, or barbican
Fardel of the sea, whose galactic flotilla make tremble,
Like an incumbent on his benefice, a hyssop
To my wounds.
                    It is past Two
World Wars: the fascia made in Rome will fester
Caucasian grapes in Germany, while the Frieslanders
Will wonder at the tea the Fuhrer sent; no holophrastic
Could dip evil's gauge so far, a nepenthe of words,
Of clementines, will make somniferous this oopher-
ectomy.

            What urtication to make our morals feel?
Go cast in Xanthian marble all that which my oeillade
jades.

1970

72

POEMS
written on certain occasions

THE WAIF POET

(for Marnie, who died aged 17, homeless and abandoned, a writer of poems of great promise)

Rife with the glad trot of dialect
Upon the public heart, her going
Shed no rhythm on the received
Opinion of the mob. She was glut –

Even outside the railings of the house
Where she conjectured with an ex-hippie
The motion of the stars, their impending
Descant in the limbo of cold aeons,

From her first fires, which flanged
The wheel of romance, as her gown trailed
And picked up mud from the night streets,
Where acid rain fell upon the buildings,

No one held her close, as shadows whispered,
Abandon her, she has too much love.

QUEEN OF HEARTS

i.m. Diana, Princess of Wales (1961-1997)

Hers, from childhood the bitter pain of tears
Dreamed to a peep-shy wedding to a Prince
Her one longing to be cherished through the years
By a lover, husband, brother: not since

The beginning of time a perfect love be found
To ease the pain of separation and of grief
She gave to others her complete round
Of compassion, love, yet was taken by a thief

To steal her image, peddle it to crowds
Make her true love of children mawkish
In death, we see her vision through such clouds
Her smile radiant, joyful, a little rakish

For hers is the Queendom, the power and the glory
Alone at the Taj Mahal, rapt in the story.

TOUCHING THE POOR

for Mother Teresa on her beatification, October 19, 2003

Her flesh recalls the beauty of her bone
Her eyes - what other centuries have known.

Radiance and joy – the alchemist's abettor
In a life of poverty, truth's only begetter -

Touching the poor, touching translucent skin
Touching in love, for the world is full of sin.

Touching in anguish, touching to save
For there's a fragrance coming from her grave;

So hope in her, whose innocence makes us feel
All that was promised for the world is real,

Haul in her net today, for life and love will meet
Eternity is crumpling posterity's time sheet

With love and joy - exactly what she willed.
She's God's friend forever, her longing is fulfilled.

THE FAREWELL TO ARMS

She says goodbye before hearing the news
Of publication she tried hard to prevent -
Like Mrs Thatcher, she has her views,
Feels such reduction printed should be sent

For review to the hireling squaw of Hell
Who, dressed in lemon, contorts to install
The phallic doubt and the parasol to sell
Clouds of nuclear fission at the Prince's ball.

What matter if the islanders lurk behind
The lens of cameras which rob the soul
The sunspots on their skin caused by a blind
Atomic monster whose parachute will not unroll

The goodies festooned in the fibre? Like their peace
wishes
She knows things can be made to look quite vicious.

FOR SPERANZA (On Oscar's birthday)

Your name means hope, wild as your nation's dreaming,
With ideas and metaphysics you were always sieving,
Your long wide skirts and your fine head teeming
For justice and peace – your ministry, your almsgiving -

Such a remarkable heart, with noted fury in debate,
For the surgeon William did not keep his vows,
The dinner table jibes, at you, his mate,
For his fruit was over-laden in the boughs -

But you had no jealousy, only wise restraint,
Up to the gate of heaven nearly wandering
With the picture of your son the world would taint,
To explain to God his singular meandering.

You were his strength - he died in victory
Over imagination's often sad reliquary.

MOTHER AND WRITER AT THE FESTIVAL

The afternoon has left me torn. In my hair
Are crow's feathers, visitant midges
And a few grey strands. The poet
Has taken his lady to the pub while

My son who interrupted his reading
On the fathers, says "I'm all right now"
Even as the poet screams "spoiled" at him. The girl
At the door asks if I'm going in again

I beg her pardon. She asks me again -
I beg her pardon. She asks if I'd prefer
To sit down. I say
Did I ask you what you prefer? She's silent.

My son stares at his water colour in its brittle
Frame. I rescue it, him, them, me, and sit.

THE MALE MUSE IN RETREAT

-"women don't exist.. apart from men thinking about
them" (attributed to Kennelly)
-

Kennelly, Kearney, Cronin and Harris
Disputed one day in the Café de Paris,
Kennelly was cheerful but the bould Cronin,
Confessed his adherents were fed up with his moanin'

While Kearney, exhibiting with exuberant glee,
European philosophy in plain ABC,
Harris, feeling appalled at reduction
Asked the kind waiter to provide Extreme Unction.

"To hell with religion, it's the fire in the belly,
You need", said the professional Kerryman, Kennelly.
The rest of the quartet were moved to declare
That women on pinheads were a new kind of prayer.

"But which of you in this difficult praxis,
Of thinking and action, can still afford taxis?"
So Kearney and Harris found they could agree
As Kennelly and Cronin shared a small pot of tea.

The truth is, since Glasnost, the old dialectic,
Which caused disputation, is nowhere near hectic,
And the once apolitical, quite apocalyptic
Wit of all four never sounded so astonishingly cryptic.

81

They vowed not to bend with the trend to put spleen on
the screen,
It quite simply dampened their meaning to mean,
They wondered how possible to still be quite zealous
Without making the Lady Good Fortune quite jealous?

But frequently put to the test on TV
They know there's nowhere like it to be, simply be.
Male writers and artists, disgraced in the past,
Might find on TV their true haven at last.

JOYCE IN NIGHTTOWN

The litanies of sacred attributes
Are the declensions in your star's slow fall
And your lyrical romance is for the brutes
Deaf to the historic footfall

Of God in the grove. The science of matter
Has given liturgy the incense of lust
And rendered intangible the good, to spatter
Beauty's white robe with a cosmic dust.

The sultry desuetude of a Jesuit school
Led you to the embrace in Nighttown
The lily-like purity of the rule
Meeting the prostitute in a dressing-gown

Your true love shows itself in opposition
The artist paring his fingernails is your position.

PRINCE CHARLES IN IRELAND

The twisted skein is stronger than the windswept fleece
And tortured twists and turns our hearts have known:
Is this process going to be a lasting peace,
Where each one loves, and each can hold their own,

A peace with your realm - not quite understood
For we live poisoned lives, in enemies and friends,
Not prefigured in our dreams of nationhood -
Now surprised by hope, and longing for leaping bends,

We are at that moment in our history,
Living with scandals in the gutter press,
Hoping curses will end, today to bless
Two islands covered in an old mystery,

The bleeding heart, the wounded in their pain,
The anodyne of grief, to love again.

WOMEN AND THE DREAM OF EUROPE
written for the European Year of the Woman 1989

He dreamed of Europa, with the feelings of a bull,
A mighty god, he saw her picking flowers
Here was a way a warring god could cull,
And keep for ever, all her golden hours,

In peace and mercy, she did yield to him,
Gave birth three-fold, then found a proper groom -
The god granted her a plane tree, for his passing whim
Went to show from conquest a love could bloom.

The trauma died, but the dream remained,
Of peace alive in her perpetual tree,
Shading her from harsh experience,
Holding fast to mercy, so to be free

Showing love was always greater when,
We promised we wouldn't go to war again.

ON REFUSING A SITTING
(for the late Edward McGuire, RHA)

I had escaped from charm school when we met
My throwaway smiles incurred no fee.
I was on a free spirit's oddessey -
So ran to ground with fine Bohemian fret -

A convent girl truant to your art -
You had the right proportion of the potion
To grant extenuation inn the notion,
If I could be recruited for the part.

But I, love-starved, was still moping
At the pangs of being my own generator,
You kept dead birds in the refrigerator
To stun the beak of history, I was hoping

The eternal feminine versus the word
Would live one day to free its own bird.

THE 'SIXTIES POEM

I reached your metaphysical penthouse on my own,
Got into bed,
Then climbed the stairs,
With you on my shoulder.

New York was far away then
Existing multifariously,
Like a colour supplement
To weigh *The Times*

Was it my need of compliment
That stole me on your clipping hawkshead
Rangers raucous angle,
And left me tied up in a hopeless,
Pocus tangle?
How did I get from the tangle to the knot?
Don't ask me,
I'm just a beautiful thought.

SIX WINDOWS

(for John McGahern)

Six windows opening out to light
Each with a wish the world be set to right

First, that the drab monologue of power
Be broken under the campanile tower

Second, that the votive bird of history
Come back again to amaze us with his mystery

Third, that the rhetoric of propagation
Begin with faith to do without a nation

Fourth, that the instance of the academy
Be honoured in a flowering knowledge tree

Fifth, that the crowd chanting at the gate
Be admitted when they doff their hate

Six, that your picture hangs in the Scholars' Gallery
Providing that the future pay your salary.

LOOKING FOR MOUNT CAMPBELL
ancestral home of " Captain Rowley"

The old woman on the bus had a voice
A happy note with a twinge of pain
A memory of Mount Campbell, to rejoice
In a summer's day with a hint of rain

Berries, apples, she had brought to the nuns
Through the double fronted door in the hall
Where the ghost of the Captain and his guns
Leaned out in search of sea, trying to recall

The touch and taste of the ocean spray
And the wooden stairs smelling of the ship
The smoke of the battle as far away
As the future hidden in an apple pip

Before she had seen the first tourist
Or the Land Commission's map showing a forest.

On being presented with THE CASE OF COINS

He wished me the wealth of Ireland in one day,
A turf-kneading bull depicted on the shilling,
A salmon leaping on the florin's way,
A stately hound not ready for the killing:

Piglets with their Mammy on the big penny
  -   was this the silken purse made from the sow's
      ear?
The horse on the half-crown, spirited as any,
The crown would wait for the wedding to my dear.

Graceful as the woodcocks on a farthing,
Where none fell to the ground without their Father's
knowledge,
He blessed me in my springtime, a little worldling
Wish I had it when I went to College!

A hare, transparent on the hungry form,
A hen with chicks, wings folding in to warm.

THE IRON LADY WEEPS

MARGARET THATCHER
Sank eight hundred men
Never to sail again
In the *General Belgrano*

When her son Mark went missing on vacation
Margaret shied away from photographer's hot flashes –
Didn't like intrusive speculation
That Mark might have found his oasis.

In the cabinet, her men shuffled with their fears –
There were pictures of wastes of sand on TV,
But the gutters of Downing Street ran with her tears
The P.M. in anguish – how could this be?

She could have bottled her tears, then, like Nero,
As she wept for love of her own creation,
But she was a mother then, and not a hero,
Temporarily retired from leading the nation.

THE STRANGE APPARITION

It's heart-scalding at my age past
The middle notch, to have to line
Up my friends and shoot them.
It's because I finally got out of bed

An invalid of fifteen years, and threw
Away the bedclothes. The social worker
Had been computing my life and found
I had more thrift than all her years at work,

That my suffering has gone to the root
Of my ideas, and put tooth on my rage
Against the world. While I did receive
Her with the profoundest compassion,

She expected me to behave like her terrier
(he's called "Buckles" and bow-wows
at the postman, she wonders if he's gay)
And be glad of any kind of attention -

But my thanks is to God, for my gift of suffering.
For the *felix culpa*, which nearly did me in.

THE ROCKY ROAD TO DUBLIN
On viewing the documentary

A Trinity student, I was editor of the magazine -
Officially, women there had a word -
I was from the West of Ireland
And was being looked upon as a dolly bird.

It was the middle of the last century, women were,
etcetera,
But we're not speaking still, unless its cross purpose,
Men were, etcetera, etcera, etcetera, etcetea,
Time for another revolution, in a cinema, I suppose,

Our contemporaries all know of the deprived
They have big jobs on account of their concern,
Their consciences fine- tuned, like the newly arrived,
But I'm still poor and needy, and I've no bra left to burn

Constitutionally banned in the Irish fit-up
Am I getting tired of being told to shut up!

IF NINE WERE SIX.. *we'd still have Jimi Hendrix)*

I was in the emergency room
I had watched him turn blue,
And I had sent for the ambulance.
It was the right thing to do.

The nurse asked me to hold him through the night
He, who had abused me for years,
People thought I was his wife.
Even blamed me for his strife.

He made it through,
He has children and grandchildren
But he still hasn't said
"Thank you."

When you're famous,
No one wants to send for the ambulance.
When you're black
White girl won't send for the crew.

A motherless child
You knew what it was to be alone,
But you needn't have died just then,
If someone knew what to do…

Sure wish it was you I saved,
Was it for revenge
That she reneged,

Sure wish it had been you ....

ON ARRIVING AT THE GREEN CONFERENCE IN LIEGE, IN 1984

The flag is lowered, then is hoisted again.
Two seagulls fly before the mast,
Eager to sport and play, behind the wake
Is a flowing reserve of deep green.

My son is sleeping in the next stack of
Lifeboats, his face offered to the skies -
The Chinese boy is looking over his shoulder
To his friend, a damson garbed girl in jeans

An augury - frozen political systems
Now alive to the measure of love and hope -
We are on an ark, and we are about to save
The world, for we make absolute sense-

The joy in my body - of imminent arrival
Is a perfect echo of the sun on the waves.

LETTER FROM AN INDIAN IN PRISON

I cannot say "I"
The person who is writing this
Is not me, but
An adjunct of the state,
My private prison officer.

I am sending this out to you
From the tyranny
Of petty officialdom
In this tired officialese
Hoping you-who-is-in-me
Will see the spirit
Cowering behind the blowtorch
Like an extinguished candle
On which an ember glows
You are the audience
Who will put that ember
Into your mouth
To cleanse yourself, and I
Am one who can speak to you
Out of suffering.

My vision has robbed my mouth
My taste is of stale dry bread
But I do not hunger
For the white man's feast
But call it famine
I do not long
To share your tap
Of water and call it truth

Only to find
A metallic taste
Where you have poisoned our inheritance
Our lands are robbed
Our children full of disease
Our animals wasted

A cup that cheers
Would need a brighter day
A day that calls us together
Is what I long for
In writing to you.

ON MY SON STEPPING ON A GARDEN SHEARS

I'm not going out tonight.

Why, Mum?

You might have a reaction.

Reaction. What's a reaction?

Do you hear the telephone – all those calls?

It's Bob.

Bob?

Bob Dylan.

He wants me to go out tonight, and I've refused.

No, Bob, no, I can't.

Really, Mum.

I may have waited 25 years for you to call, but still, I'm
not going out with you tonight.

Even if he rings back?

Even if he rings back five times.

I'll say, I'm striking you off my list, Bob

You could have been the one, in these missionary times,.
But I'm not pledging my time, this time.

Go on, said my son, picking at the large piece of
Elastoplast stuck to his jaw.

No, I said, not even Bob.

What about the Pope? he asked.

Even if he comes here in his sandals,

Gathering his cassock as he climbs the stairs to you,

Holding in his hand a little ciborium from Rome
With the host -

When is Jesus going to break out of the tablet, Mum?

When you stop sucking your thumb

But taking the host, you might be cured forever - of the
years you children have spent, outstretched on the big
cross, petrol fumes and poisoned food..

Will the Pope read a story, Mum?

Maybe, but he does not like fairy tales, nor the truth of
women's experience

No, I'd rather you went out with Bob Dylan - he looks as
if he's been in the cave of time.

IN THE GARDEN OF CONTEMPLATION AND BEAUTY

For my own child, my love and sudden flower
My fruitful hope weighed down with my despair
I'll have to give away my greatest hour
To those who reckon not each counted hair

The little cheek, the expression in the eye
Is mine, yet not my own, just loaned to me
I am bereft of my life's most precious sigh
The sound of my own child who groaned in me

If I'm oppressed, I'm not just passing on
Ignorance, prejudice learned from the hard of heart
I scrub the stairs, my body weighs a ton
My way is perfect love, it's yours to start -

He'll meet us at the tomb, and in His hand,
My work-worn posy, my beautiful ampersand.

MOTHER

for Nora (1911-1977) on her birthday

Compared to a lady, her flower of selfhood wilted
Consort to an artist, she became an odalisque
Wife to a husband, she scratched beneath his feet
Mother to her sons, she offered life's blood
Model for her daughters, she sanctioned them to tears
I learned to love her, the adolescent who had been
Sent to cousins – acolytes for priesthood
She sacrificed her youth at their altar
And sang her songs on ingressive breaths
While they remarked on tiny insect deaths

I divine her spirit stifled in the bloom
Rough hands that could at times wreak havoc
Over my un-tonsured maiden's head
Her veined legs and her bags of shopping
Sometimes I wished her and myself dead

She gave me life, a gift which leaves me room
A mother now, I the weft of loom
Each time I sense a rancour outwards boom
I hold the rage, it was her fierce ransom
Bought me the freedom I scarce had to win.

Betrayal into Origin

Dancing & Revolution in the 60's

When from dark error's subjugation
My words of passionate exhortation
Have wrenched thy fainting spirit free,
Then writhing forth in thy affliction,
Thou didst recall, with malediction,
Those who had encompassed thee..
Nekrassov

1ˢᵗ prizewinner

Scottish Open International Poetry Competition
1996

In referring to individual stanzas, please refer to page number, and then stanza A and B.

The blue spread of heaven lay upon the sea:
She dreamed of Diarmuid's horsemen in the hills
Escorting Aoife to be wed, and victory
In Strongbow's arrows penetrating thrills.
On the green heap of Wicklow she poured tea
For her lover and she spread among their pills,
In truth, experience can borrow words on spree
And desecrate the harbour of our wills:
No foreign hand will ever cup my breast,
Make of our bitter country a ribald jest.

A traitor is a term beyond contempt,
Betrayal a seepage of the blood:
In bonds of trust she lay, her head content -
Cultural impurity was not what they would
Bestow on the children, though the rent
Of space and time disinherit good -
Their vision, robbed of right intent,
But redeeming imperfection by the flood
Of joy that was his hand caressing
Where she had begun her undressing.

Yet caresses build up a round of sense
Once walked upon, a highway for a life,
And bonds are made of fingers twining dense
Chords in the soul. A woman made wife
In breach of tradition will hunt the pence
Forever in the kitchen till the strife
Breaks over her head like tillage over tents;
And brute growth can make her body rife -
A graveyard of promises with white stones
A dinner plate piled high with brittle bones.

A lover is a fantasy in time
In which the real chases its own tail;
Exhausted heads puzzle out the rhyme
And the children tumble down the hill with pail.
Their crowns are hurt and love's sweet reckless mime
Is a surly reader of page 3, a body for sale
A legal contract that shops short of crime.
She thought she was free, and now a nail
Scourges her flesh in bondage to her clan;
For love's a paved garden and a man.

And still, in the repast of the flesh
The ghost at the banquet pitched his head
Upon the plate of warm desire, a fresh
Bouquet falling. Flowers white and red
Scented their Moorish heaven like a mesh
Of truth upon a fiction. The dead
Speak little yet the ghost gave prec-
ious leaving like a splinter she had shed
Upon the cross they had woven out of song,
To tell their hearers that they did no wrong.

How could they not but love? - lover spoke so kind -
They who were righting wrongs could know the truth:
His words hurled like stones upon her mind,
Brought to a sudden end protracted youth.
See how the grass bends with the wind
Yet he received her words with no ruth,
And building justice, brick by brick, was blind
To the wild tree of creation, yet uncouth,
As the menaced souls of people in a slum
Destroy the garden that the rent men plumb.

The nationhood of woman at a loss
Can emphasise its own bequesting spirit,
But founded in blood, is blameless in the toss
Of beauty, which the lands inherit:
God-given gift sold cheaply to emboss
A brazen rouge which you name as merit -
A banner, flag, epitome of joss
Which in fake ardour a new man will ferret
To taint the ages with a hint of mystery
That you were real and had a place in history.

How did she give herself his tarnished role,
How did any man cheat his way to kill,
How did his lust linger on her soul
Against her instinct, passion, mind and will?
How was she branded with predestined scroll
When she loved God and wanted him to fill
All her days with longing for the whole
To be at one with Him, and mercy still?
How could she be set against her own
Her body, mind and spirit so alone?

In Lawrence's church in the hurdle-forded town
The Pope had issued a severe decree;
The Celtic church avowed a papal frown
Adrian ran his bull in a spirited See.
The way was narrow and of no renown.
A *poitin* still was banned by Saxon fee.
Three spirals grew into a twisted noun:
Name-giving and forsaking women free.
By then the unruly place had invented its own ale,
And imprisoned its own members inside the Pale.

The centuries rolled by slowly with a crust
Of meaning underneath the layers of scorn:
The land was covered as a Celtic rust
In truth and knowledge many a poet was born:
Each prophet stoned who had a mission to dust.
Men and women were sold for strangers' corn,
While they did sell their spirit on what they sussed
And laid their youngsters on the slab with porn -
A hatred for their own - the die was cast
By a mob of crazed politicos from Belfast.

For ballads there was none to beat the fair
City in its hunger for the dark,
Before Darwin took his monkeys for a rare
Saunter in the Phoenix Park.
However, when it came to passions bare
Of sentiment and nation in a quark
We went to jail, to die from a dare -
We preferred death to living in the ark.
We took a leap from being puritan to a faith,
And left our own as loveless as a wraith.

In the dim days when dancing was a sin,
Convent girls were taught they mustn't swagger,
Or fade to where the walls and hopes were thin -
- the era of rock'n'roll and Mick Jagger
Rushed in, and arguments who would win
For women's flowering: for those who sought to gag her
Salvation was the only goal, and the distant din
Of wars and rumours made rich the carpetbagger,
Whose daughters in the convent school for wives
Had as their daily text quiet cloistered lives.

The holy retreat where the priest sermonised to warn
Against the world, the flesh, and the devil:
He was among girls he was born to scorn
And his picture of hell showed many a revel.
In his fiery rhetoric he mixed with the porn
The fright of imagination where he could level
Old charges on the girls, in original sin born -
Girls innocent for a while, but boys would dishevel
These neat heads: a boy who at a glance
Could turn into a fiery devil at a dance.

She left school with her honours intact:
The boys nearly fainted when they heard.
Most men had liked to pontificate
Making her dismissed as a brainy bird.
Male bonding was a heavy syndicate
An intelligent woman was something too absurd -
Her job would be to type his letters in triplicate
And not her own stuff, for such was woman's word.
She lost her dream of equality in the office,
The daytime world powerless and loveless.

So-given the convent as a bourgeois dream
Of advantageous desire or prudent concupiscence
She would have to search for love in a different scheme
And opted then for dancing's munificence.
Such was her skill with movement she would redeem
Those days when all was boring competence
In transcribing notes, she'd have independence and
esteem,
Then night-time and a lover's magnificence
True love and companion to be sought in a daze
Of mirrors, powder, and the ballroom craze.

In her dream, the shadow and the light
Tireless in motion,   a perpetual star
Twinkling with love, and incandescent, bright
Like the difference between male and female are
With luminous numinous form, each man a sight
Of the deity, as the cosmos each day dances far
Into infinity with the many and the one, right
On a course of complexity, yet on a par
With justice, beauty and salvation -
Dancing became her inspiration.

This was before the celebrated mini,
Before women's lib scored an own goal:
She went dancing every night, it was her destiny,
Her prayer, her contact with the over-soul.
One partner had wet hair, it was stiff and satiny
He was the one who asked her to do the stroll:
Another one was tall, another skinny,
As they twisted, then went on to rock 'n' roll.
The ballroom was a class and tribal hunt
With conversation like a daring high wire stunt.

One had pimples, and bright red curly locks
His face was pasty, yet he was romancing
He had bright button eyes with laugh line shocks
And a motor bike better than any Lansing.
He wore check trousers and bright yellow socks.
He looked at her as if she were enhancing
His life at week-ends, scrambling over rocks,
And with him be daring, be all-chancing.
This date was forbidden by her mother -
He was dangerous, and not worth the bother.

She dreamt of her ideal, and how she would kiss
This substance of all shadow, her perfect man -
He'd be tall, dark and handsome, to bring bliss
And grace so natural, perhaps a little tan:
She'd know him at once, she'd never miss
This man to turn everyone else to an also-ran:
She'd know love at last, and it was this conviction
That made her persist as true love's fan.
She lived in the dance, an unconscious chaotic
Will to turn her whole life erotic.

She saw him down the splendour of the night,
The face for which master painters might have sighed
And his hair lay on his collar, she had the right
Impulse to hold – yet was frantic inside.
They danced each Saturday, it was a rite
Private and holy like religion that had vied
For her their souls, whose goodness like a light
Came with desire as insistent as the tide:
He wanted to make love but she forbade
What her mother and the nuns described as *bad.*

Lie down, my love, on the grass
And we won't give a tupenny straw or feather
For what old women think – I will pass
On the bad and the good – now there's a tether
To tie the thinker in. The mass
Of people will never know love, or whether
It's true or false. I would bet my cuirass
Kings would change places with us together -
Love me now, don't leave me half-way there.
She said: *Desire is a banister with no stair.*

You're suffering from too much education
Thinking like you, I'd rather go spare
Schooling women, next the waste of nation
The next generation will be quare.
So spoke her delight, her inspiration
He said she'd ruin her coat on the grass there
What could she do to give him consolation
But her dream was of life, and his so bare
To be left at the crossroads of never
Was the payment for comely maidens who were clever.

So, like a ship, which leaves a wall of foam,
The dance was more precious than before:
His shadow, his tousled hair and his comb
Projecting from his pocket like male lore
To match the red handkerchief, a poem
Of bleeding streets and dingy record store;
And when his denial hit home
She was wounded and scorned to her very core -
For he saw in her only a stereotypical woman,
One who loved beauty that was common.

So her love for a young man, so obdurate -
Her first, was pure, and had come to grief,
And in that painful space he left a spirit
Which fed upon her treasures like a thief.
This young man, who tried to inspirit
Beauty, who forced a dream within her brief
Concourse with him, how he could dispirit
Not just her yearning for love, but her belief
In herself – heart and mind failed, like a widow:
As if his death was real, and he a Gaelic Bushido.

She mourned for him in months of crazy dancing,
The Beatles' songs were climbing up the charts,
Her pride got a right sore gut-lancing
And now she was immune from Cupid's darts.
One night, a zombie, she was prancing
When a rich young man succumbed to her arts,
He asked her to dance, and he was chancing
His neck, his wallet, and his fragile parts:
She said yes, and he was captivated
He was tired of spoiled girls who titillated.

He swept her round the floor in virile leaps,
Her hair swept in a dotted scarf, her god
May have left her in mirrored broken heaps
But still there were dreams in the rumpled sod
 - Ireland. She was young, yet she who reaps
Before she sows, can find a barren rod
Of angels' tears, dried up, and seeps
With goodness, as if useless, for a hod
Whose bricks will build an easier tomorrow -
If the dancing girl forget her sorrow.

She liked him, he was kind, he was nice -
A little portly, but with outline sleek -
He had money, but he had not yet a vice
And he was unpretentious and quite meek.
It could be, in a few months, that rice
Would be thrown at her in a shower of pique
By wedding guests who envied the thick slice
Of cake she'd captured: a god, not Greek,
But rich as Croesus - and to boot
She wouldn't have to worry about loot.

But think she did, and then she grew quite worried:
The world is badly divided, said her mother -
The rich man drove her home, and raindrops slurried^{ther}
Down the windowpane where they had found each o
His gloves at the wheel, he wasn't hurried
But he gave her time to think, it was no bother
What bride could be seen to be flurried
With such riches in store, bad luck to smother
Yet it would take away the rights of her brothers
If she choose a rich man above the others.

Her pals teased her – the big Mercedes
Put a block of black around her heart -
No more could she sing of her free days
If she were to be bought from the start:
He could be a life-buoy in the sea days
With her heart anchored in the dart
Of social approval, far from the glee days
Of beauty and the beast, market and mart,
When a child would be born to a new dynasty
Who might sleep to the lullaby of property.

The rich young man was wounded in his pride:
Sizzling schemes of run down city housing,
Love frozen in an architectural tide,
And high rise flats where the culture's dowsing
Brought from the town's entrails a wide
Brief on folkloric custom and carousing.
In urban squalor people lived and died
Now they would be subject to delousing;
In concrete, with plastic and with iron girders
Was flattened out beauty with green murders.

No park was planned to make the people easy,
No blade of grass grew from the concrete floor,
Nor truth offer shade to the sick and queasy,
Nor flower scent the valley of the poor.
The sky was blotted out like a speak-easy.
What could grow in such an urban sore?
How easy for the builder to be breezy,
In his summer lawn planning a score
Of flats in towers looming to the sky,
Clustered like battalions for children's hearts to die.

And she was wounded by something very slight
A snobbery which made her sort of cringe -
His inability, to say with friends, "goodnight".
There was no one to listen to her twinge
Of dismay and disbelief in the new site,
Only parties where planners would binge
On agreeing that might was right
For her a community would hinge
On the lack of space, so detrimental
People labelled sad, bad and *mental.*

His family were no different, had traded in
Africa, and had page slave wages to blacks
To ensure the white world was barricaded in
With privilege, guns, dogs, and right-wing hacks.
It was a river of sorrow to be waded in.
No opportunity, and for what oppression lacks -
Freedom, dignity - Her tears cascaded in
The century's preference for no-gooding quacks:
She left the rich man at her father's gate,
Rejoicing in her singularly sinless state.

Injustice often buries fear in the throat
Fear to speak, to act out our liberty.
She thought of truth, an ever-butting goat
But where was inspiration in liquidity?
What jewels and what many coloured coat
Are bartered every day for mean cupidity -
The flexing roll of muscles for a banknote -
- Men between torture and stupidity -
She had loved the poor so intensely
She couldn't care for the rich man immensely.

The divine wind had left her. Alone
And in the abyss, she, bereft bird
Trembled with fear, and the loan
On love's meaning was absurd.
At the funeral of love, an infinity was blown
By mourners of romance, and now was heard
Deciphering her pain in ceaseless moan.
All for want of love, when a single word
Could have given so much, perhaps a hope,
That she could face hard questions, and cope.

Better seize the root that spreads decay
Than glitter emptiness upon the poor:
An ordinary man with nothing to say
Is better on the land than on the shore -
When the foundation is rotten who can pay
For reconstruction of the temple pure
When dreams are made of gold, who can pray?
Or when they're of mud, a wattle door.
A woman thus hated has no fee
Cannot be bought, is straight despised and free.

So she employed a logician
To squash forever the poet in her soul -
In Dublin the calling of magician
Made redundant her mother-martyr role.
As she teased out with care each word's inflection
At the exact nature of dearth and dole,
The pain of poverty upon reflection
She sought the cure, the universe to thole:
As falling through history, a recalcitrant demon
Meets with the quintessential Irish lemon.

For theirs was a fevered generation:
The world stood by - an ashen tomb -
Eight minutes away from ending - in desperation
They made a pact together to face down doom.
"Go forth and multiply" a desecration
So life became a fruitless vacuum;
With quotes from revolution, and dissolution.
They were entangled in the Celtic gloom.
Yet to miss her one true love, the greatest fear
According to the pop songs poured in her ear.

A bride without a veil, no photos taken:
She was straightaway deserted, without a tribe,
All beauty, love and happiness forsaken,
No dowry – for that was considered bribe.
Legally bound, part of an idle squadron
Absolved from work, a mute female scribe,
She somehow had to bring home the bacon
Dry her tears alone after each cruel jibe,
He enjoyed a licence to shirk,
The Constitution took away her right to work.

Sexualised - an abandoned bride
In Christian eyes, rotten to the core -
Yet there may have been a noble one in pride
Who wouldn't brand woman as a whore
Who would, a comrade by her side,
Win a world for the dreams of the poor.
One like herself, whose exterior belied
A really splendid soul, where she could pour
The finest ideal of a nation's flower,
Like a lily in a desperate hour.

In class, determinism, and the proletariat
She was now the prey of the Marxist hunt -
In her wildest thought was now a lariat
Which reduced all expression to a grunt.
Exiled, he compared her to Iscariot,
Everyone in Ireland a puerile runt
Who had refused the poor, and his chariot
A band-wagon he mounted for a stunt
To show how equality was made,
The highest with the poorest would be paid.

One equal in vision, and in conceit
Decided immediately they were hitched,
With sex an exploration, a hot treat
To sustain them if the ideal were ditched:
But now it was to turn to cold meat
When reason against passion would be pitched
In objectivity, and their hearts beat
A rhythm in which they could be stitched -
With disillusionment, they were committed,
When they learnt all, that their parts fitted.

Her part un-written, unofficially summarised.
A woman never bought is without spice -
And then those rumours that she paralysed
Each male libido with her cunning guise.
Ireland, a hag, or prostitute symbolised
A virgin tarnished, though she had no price -
But prices must through shame be realised,
When fire meets fire, or ice encounters ice -
The bit between her teeth never sweeter
To those who lay astride to harm and cheat her.

Belfast, your sons come out from sombre morgues
Your courage rains down the streets of the South;
You sing your dirges of inflated torcs
Your gutters running with a bloodied mouth.
We choke on you, a part of archeology,
Giants and rings to show we're one nation.
Our common heritage is not swapology,
But is in fact a poor fool's halting station.
Eclectic, but diverse until death
Our love like living blooms upon a wreath.

The original traitors from the sea
Came to settle in the Fifth invasion,
Before these we learned to bend our knee
Now again there is our tribal fascination,
With stories, geasa, and *foras imbai*
Like our dreams, we grew to a gross gestation -
Our labyrinthine structures, our devastation
With language, and flags, and symbols going free,
The Celtic cross, the Sheila, and the banished snake
Made exiles of us all, our thirst to slake.

But freedom is a kind of strange inversion,
It gives power to a new republic's eye -
Which saw istself foredestined to dispersion
Could not harbour dissent, that's the why
A caustic lute needed no diversion
And storied cant forbade the inner cry
Who would believe a woman's immersion
In a culture where there was no why
The instant it was uttered, a fell proof,
Dismissal the Creator's own reproof.

First the Bishop disavows his son,
Fails to mention he had sinned with Annie:
The government free criminals on the run
And re-arrest all who can't be canny.
Priests and brothers have with kids their fun,
Abuse a sacred trust while playing Nanny -
The newspapers squeeze life into a pun,
To satisfy the few, and hurt the many.
Women were given poisonous anti-D
While a doctor operated who carried HIV.

Under the afterglow, a woman he could use,
Scoring a blue trail for the Belfast streets -
God's ugly city, daily peruse
The gospel of the sun and shot red meats.
Upon the Milky Way a bloody pattern
Slipped to the umbrella of this lover's guise:
His queen, Real Life, was a slattern
As the blue evening skies became night skies.
In truth, he was a lover of pulp fiction
Who thought true love lay in body friction.

His was the word, hers was the tender flesh,
He would give reality its shape -
He would hammer out meaning in a mesh
Of language, and her phrases he would tape.
Her ideals, intentions, fresh
As the auburn knob which lay upon her nape.
Exploring and exploiting he would thresh
The seeds of knowledge for the world to gape
At him, her admiring and adoring mentor:
He god-like, progenitor, inventor.

Mean streets were not encouraging of valour,
There was money to be made in being the card:
At funerals, he could buy and sell her,
Life impossible, dealing way too hard.
A rabble rousing bouquet to the mob,
A torn-asunder ideal soaked in virulence,
The mall, the larder and the upstart gob
Declaiming hatred of women as a penance -
His cant to believe a Southern lass –
Who was ignorant of what would come to pass.

Fresh from the pageant of his own esteem,
He failed to notice that she had a quibble -
She had believed she could work with a team,
But her country's longing was for a silent sibyl.
Woman an object, a property to cream
And now she was just a patriot's dibble -
Her imagination and her mind began to teem
And so she began at last to scribble -
She decided to give herself to writing verses
To distract her from her country's curses.

She became the source of instant fame
There was much general celebration -
She found she had a calling in which untame
Passions like hers were scholarly dissertation -
At poetry circles each week she would declaim
Her lines of poetry to the general population,
To him her voice of nationhood was lame
And looked on it as a kind of desecration,
Once more she had betrayed the country's wrong
And he alone judged fit to sing the song.

So for Ireland's sake they lay upon the bog,
North and South disputing ancestry -
Upon their joint escutcheon a raging dog
To cheat them of their little posterity -
They joined, they raced, they tumbled to their thrills
She came oblivious of any danger
As she lay obedient to God's mills
Grinding narrowly, he became a stranger.
And as for her, she simply hadn't reckoned
What resulted in being pinned down for a second.

Pain has no price quite like that of pleasure,
The Belfast man now scrounged for a view.
As she lay there, a violated treasure,
Her changing mores, like a diphthong screw,
To give her the proper Irish measure.
She was now the elect, one of the suffering few
Which he could ponder in his sensuous leisure
To view, in *flagrante,* what he already knew:
Anger and betrayal would behove him
For she had written that she didn't love him.

.

You can be blessed, knowing the wrong you did,
You can celebrate difference till the cows come home,
But can you attribute morality to a skid
Of fashion in a tablet damned by Rome?
Can you say you were led by your own lid
Forgot to swallow something on writing a poem,
This led to the destruction of your own kid,
And the contemplation of many a legal tome.
For truth and morality went out the door
When she didn't fit his precept of male lore.

Between the private and the public she was trapped,
On the edge of the ideal and the real.
The state her independent soul had sapped
And the ethics wouldn't let the personal feel.
Something within her spirit now had snapped
Yet she refused to let her fear congeal,
And wrote of her love of the Other, still untapped,
But stopped from the start, to reveal.
That the fault that lay not in her, but in her nation
For making in gender such discrimination.

Fate has its decree and love is bound
By infinite odd and mighty circumstance:
Whoever we may be, we are as found -
A vague entry to the lane of happenstance;
Entwined with neighbours, we may be round
As lovers, be fools, or genius with a chance
When emotion is transformed into sound
And beauty dwells within a formal dance.
For we love one another as we will,
The thought is frightening that we can kill.

So can we love where we most despise?
Can envy flower without pain?
Is it called love when jealousy's a guise
To understand our difference in the rain?
A friend forever, it's a lifetime prize
But if we're robbed in romancer's lane
We may as well forget the enterprise
A heart broken, and nothing to gain.
To try to live in beauty and truth until we die
Gets no answer down the centuries, asking why.

She was not left to right the wrong,
So conception became conspiracy -
An outrage on a free soul left too long
The price so high, it ransacked liberty.
To nourish what was a source of depravity
Was to give life to a tattered song,
The price so high it ransacked liberty -
A being to whom no one could belong
Except to be an outright travesty.
So she did the necessary, and sold the good,
Rent unborn limbs and pillaged motherhood.

The treasures of the past, of golden splendour,
Are monuments of mind's heroic passion -
By now she had indicated her surrender
To doctrines that were going out of fashion,
Life and equality, a nail to rend her
As they peeked beneath her skirts in a session
With her own flesh they can damn her mend her
Her beauty now in a distinct recession:
The worst to hear now, that a child is "heaven sent"
Out of which comes this passing monument.

The thought of killing wasn't very central:
Dehumanised, she couldn't feel its pain
Until afterwards, her head split, elemental
To shoot her daily, bullets in the brain.
She was defeated, now a video rental
Is selling her beauty to another Cain.
In circumstances, it was all so fragmental
She had given herself with nothing to gain,
And a baby, whose life she had to smother
Because she wasn't just another mother.

So ended the life of a precious child,
No justification for the ghastly deed
What now of independence or injustice wild
Just an uncouth admission of a raw willed need.
She was a biochemical property, was riled
That he should betray her dream and screed
And put it down to pills, which now were filed
Like an admission on the news reports of greed,
That she was a thing, an object to be screwed
Like living hell among the rude and nude.

Because she had been left out of the story,
Then believed equality was a point of reference,
To which they could return in sunset's glory,
To illustrate her delicacy and deference,
He had absconded from their future's hoary
Bright winter of her fertile evanescence,
Now he wrote diatribe like a Tory
Who had invented surrender to tumescence,
To stop life which wasn't hers to begin with
So without sin, he found someone new to sin with.

Something so quickly done was his disclaimer,
Something so agonising, her retreat,
In shock, it became a way to tame her
In recollection, she was just a piece of meat.
The boat suspended all who now could claim her
Her life was put on hold, so to greet
Her family, who didn't mean to maim her
With baby photos, bootees with no feet,
Empty prams in hallways with chipped plaster,
Showed clearly that her life was a disaster.

She had nightmares when a train went whoosh,
And swept a baby carriage along the rails -
She ran through carriages, a vision *louche*
Screamed for her baby, which an empty pram assails
The bullet gone, what's left is a cartouche
Where death scrawled in haste of life, which fails
Even when curtains close upon a couch,
The whole train hears her screams and wails:
Her baby gone forever, with a mad scream
Because the reality upset the dream.

If only she had been herself to start with,
Instead of indeterminacy and no regard
Had found love , horse and cart with
The aloneness of being a woman bard.
Trapped in definition, no heart with
To persuade that her case was very hard.
Make her an example, and part with
Her sanity, like the deck's last card -
His ambition had brought her to here;
Life contingent on what she held dear.

Somehow, it seemed, that dreams were not for her
She and her child, somehow, had to pay -
Mother a womb-tomb, each behaved like a cur
Feeding on darkness, over which to prey:
The old sow and her farrow a real slur,
Not just literary caveat, fashioned to lay
Upon inverted debts, and thus incur
The wrath of God in a single day.
It was only a simple operation,
Carried out on women of poor station.

You can ask, how did she do such a thing,
Stamp on her baby's face and rent the limbs
When the child is the brightest jewel in the ring
Even with earth's exquisitely blue rims,
Her infinite self, a spirit from the King
And Lord of Love, but a robber never skims,
But takes the centre of the bowl to sing
In praises of her soul's imperious whims.
Now you understand it is difficult to bless.
Life, when heart and soul must here regress.

The rift between them a chasm as before,
Her mother's servitude and sacrifice,
Gripping on nothing, the person was no more,
She had become a means: it wasn't nice -
Endless as the waves on the pebbled shore
Leading to selflessness, another vice,
So daughter saw in mother an old sore,
A handle to a hand of bad advice;
In the state of nature, there was corruption
Or an evil eye ready for eruption.

Now she answers that she cannot allow
For the love and beauty in her heart
Be a travesty and the substance of a row,
Like unity in her country, torn apart.
She held grace like a necklace on the bow
Of a dazzling ship bedecked with light and art,
But she couldn't accept involuntarily to endow
Another with life, while playing the observer's part
So they moved in with a license and a twist
To add killing after killing to the list.

Thousands of seedlings left to die alone,
On a Petrie dish, whose first cry is their last -
This lesser of two evils heard to moan
For a second, before the knife is cast
Into the womb, and the two now well known
In the ache of the abyss. The executioner's vast
Indifference to each solitary groan
As ever an innocent head to death is passed
For unborn life we have no right to smother
For joy and hope die, and the love of mother.

Reckon not these ways and be an artist,
Where all is justified, every blessed sin -
To live the life, and be diurnal chartist
Of daily killing, and the experience revel in,
Make the world a shroud, in order to subsist
Be deaf to music and the din
Of unborn babes murdered by a fascist
Endeavour to make the whole fit in:
Young and wronged, the little creature
Instead of life, will in a story feature.

How can it be that in our troubled history
There are still no stories of the unborn?
How in the enfolding of this mystery
Are womanhood and nationhood torn?
As they lay above the sea, in their consistory
Of hope to shield them from the ages' scorn,
That its rack and blood stained bistoury
Would vanish in the golden heads of corn:
The land, our love, our unutterable lacks
Bringing us the grave, our wanton hacks.

If love's the word, how come such disunion
Led to relentless and unceasing gripe?
Bad faith led to a false communion
Which was loved only for its hype.
Belief that mother and child need re-union
With gifts and auguries before they are ripe,
He took the run and bundled to the Union
Where he swore in triplicate, in type,
For her ambition, she got the man's rate
For proving she was equal, and his surrogate.

Can you imagine how the centuries' trust
Enfolded Nature like a beauty given
To the heart of man and woman, a crust
On which the eternal word is leaven!
Beauty and truth were green, when the dust
Of cities arose above the plain, a heaven
Was lost. The sobs and thralls of lust
In the oiled machine of love and earth riven,
And on this broken wing of song a pain
Lay on the heart like fermenting grain.

So a countryman comes to the city
Idolising woman as the land -
To bring forth children without pity
And the harsh town is made of yellow sand
Money buys silence, and an arcane ditty
Will supplant the ballads, to be panned
By sophisticates whose paper bond is witty
Epigram on abstract wealth, and banned
In the new country, a connection to the soil
Whose perfume undergoes the work of toil.

Yet our tarnished history gives such a story –
Medhbh with her friendly thighs and stamping bull
Emer discreet with mischief before the hoary
Compliments of her suitor who would cull
Ireland's forests before he traduce the glory
Of her breasts, and territorial claims annul.
For three thousand years, Nationalist and Tory
Fought for our north-east corner, for a hull
Ever resurgent on the bloody sea,
And turned us into traitors, you and me.

So we are born to secrets, age to age
Some shot at funerals buying silences to spring
In the music of our hearers' grief and rage,
The hope one day, like her, who cling
To song as the expression of her mage.
One day there'll be a perfect ring
As the heeded sayings of a sage
As warrior women to their babies sing
Born from where they were torn and sundered
From that first dream where we freely wandered.

It may be that the hunger still has grip
As the city slickers, rooted in obscurity
Wither like the haw, whose bright red tip
Lost in the seasonless clay of insecurity -
The petty clerkships and the unctuous lip
Keeps crumbs on the palate while the purity
Of good languishes at the cross- roads, a pip
To be spat out at futurity -
Ciphers on a banker's ledger sheet
Zeroed figures replacing a stack of wheat.

The bogs which guard the heritage of the past
Today yielded up a ton of butter -
The wicker-wrapped corbel, like an interest, cast
On living truths which we have lost; to splutter
Down the ages like a Scholiast
Whose ornate calligraphy is the abstract stutter
Of people's shame, disowning heritage for caste,
And intricate feeling for a slavey's mutter -
The sharp distinctions of a race and age
Frozen in complicated beauty on the page.

fin

The Wake of Wonder

A sequence on love - political, personal, sexual and ecological, asking questions on the possibility of saving the world, and the whole damn thing..

As we gaze from the portals of the past, to wake the dead, and look to the future, for the awakening of spirit..

Written in 1987, reflecting on the events of the 'sixties, seventies, and eighties..

Prize winner in the Scottish International Open Poetry Competition, 1997.

ONE – *as our heroine contemplates her pregnancy, she asks herself how the democratic ideal, birth in the log cabin, and death in the White House, is going to affect her chances..*

A cabin low in roof, and in estate,
Does not by way of telling, celebrate.
But is an emblem of the age, ambition's tale
To wonder at, while others tend to rail,
At fortune's glissandos, or romancer's doom
Which brought the haberdasher on her honeymoon
And left a pile of nappies on the line..
And the listener, questioning what tine
Had first quashed her dawn's rococo chorus
With loud wails, and tiresome *deoch-a-dorais*
A never departing guest from the ceremony,
But hidden from the eyes of patrimony,
Though present when the register was signed –
How could this be answered, when love is blind?

The row of nappies is perfunctory
    -    a mere decoration, and quite literary –
In truth, her mind was often with them strewn
While she wept copious tears on the honeymoon.
'Twas spent in Liverpool, and at card games
Where guttural swearing was the norm, and shames
What the Beatles started in the Cavern,
While she tried to drink the waters of Malvern,
To purify the dedicate zygote
Who clung to her body with untimely rote,
While she counted days, staring at the ceiling.
Was the birth to come, destruction, or a healing?
He didn't care. With law he had impounded her,
And with his swift philosophies confounded her.

147

As she lay striated on the blanket
Of day, which crept around her like a junket
Of unappeased trifles, adding up to gluttony,
She thought her best defence was surely mutiny.
She sat, wall-eyed, at Pontoon and at Poke
As though what was on her person was a joker,
At twenty-five (a guess) was struck with boredom,
And like an aged Queen, surveyed her whoredom.
Her abandoned virginity was like a palimpsest
On which was written – *Act, or Turn to Dust* –
With joined hands in love-locked bands to decipher
The code of the universe. Love was rifer
There than in the card-game, had time to ooze
Out of the gim-cracked days a lozenged ruse.

For she, a fresh-faced girl, had worn a mask,
Which made telling the truth itself a simple task
Open to the window of her mind
She left her horse, like common sense, behind.
She thought she could, with experience, be tender,
If body subsequently reduced soul to cinder,
So not deterred by his strong covenant
Became in Liverpool, a hierophant.
But this knowledge her spirit subdued
To body and bone, was just dust. Renewed
Its pact with death. And through that death
A newborn possibility, birth and a wreath,
Abraxus at nightfall, Adam and Eve
Once more biting the apple. Again to grieve.

Love is blind when people go astray

And flourish, but couples have to pay
Now she had lost for good the right to work
Save in the house, nor dirty dishes shirk.
Lincoln, it seemed, had set a good example –
From the candy store to the chapel is a sample –
She thought of her child, and how she had spent
Her dreams of happiness ending in discontent
As if she was turned to waste, boring and thriftless
As lovers they were spent, their love was shiftless.
As she contemplated why she had to marry,
Playing poker with Tom and Dick and Harry,
She looked at the essence of her journey
Felt she had overspent on patrimony.

The talk was of politics. The day would come
When everyone would have a good income,
Stealing, lies, dishonesty, would be no more
Woman rescued, to a housewife from a whore,
Given a place at work, but keeping essence
As assistant when coming to tumescence -
Priapus dethroned. He talked of climax
As if sitting on a pile of thumbtacks –
Grim hostelry of youth, their posters became
Realer to them than her slip-shod brain
Which passed critical notes like "saturated"
Whenever his ideas were aerated –
Especially when dialectics was the answer
To rid the world of its overwhelming cancer.

Capitalism, of course, was chief among crimes,
Having its apogee in modern times,

From feudalism, the infant capital's delight
To every single form of mannered spite.
It was to be seen in the corruption of the boss,
Who for the workers never gave a toss,
It could be seen in the frown of the schoolmaster,
Whose face still spelt for his pupils a disaster,
Of course, glaringly obvious it was women,
Were up to their oxters, sinking, swimming,
In the foul effluent that was the male ego..
Borrowed from the master class of long ago..
Reducing all to slave.. ergo, the shovel
Without which an epic is just a novel.

TWO – *our heroine thinks on how democracy in ascendant from the cabin to the White House, depends on the role of education*

A beginning, a middle, and an end
Saves the reader from going around the bend,
The chronic lessee of the formless plot,
Discovers matters in a crooked knot.
So far, we have started this verse novel,
To find literary provenance in a hovel,
We mentioned 19th century philosophy
While the reader no doubt sipped her tea –
A beverage thrown in for illustration –
On how incident works relevant to our station.
How is tea germane? The reader asks,
This writer is neglecting serious tasks,
Sequence, logic, development of story
The cast are already dyed in a beverage hoary.

A family is where the strife began –
A city aspirant, a countryman,

Resolved to earn his living in the town
And see his offspring sport a master's gown.
With rough hands he carved out their destiny
Swearing each of his progeny be free
From sweating toil and back-breaking work,
Which he himself, a family man, didn't shirk.
Great to his proud hope, the children grew
And quarrelled wholesomely on what they knew
Their teachers said they were extremely bright
They didn't snuff the candle till the light
Of the street faded at dawn, prodigious learners
Soon to be converted into earners.

Diligence now reared its ruffled head
Axioms into brains were sped, and spread,
Equations, quadratic and simple
Were the accompaniment to the teenage pimple,
Paradigms, abstracts, and pot resume
Were ingested with the bacon and the tay,
Latin was copiously inflexed,
And never were these heroic efforts vexed
By unseen translations – and Irish, too
The Celtic story where all myths are true.
And from there was much diversion
And how to make the appropriate conversion
From outlawed bard, to peasant turned a pedant,
There was hardly any antecedent.

A tangled tough lot, ready
To prove Darwin right. Said he
Survival of the fittest? He was right.
It only went to prove the apple bite

Had taken place before her honeymoon
Now with Nature, she had the devil's boon.
In actual fact, the dissonance of matter
Showed her distance from God no mere splatter
But evidence of mankind's dark affliction
Which occurred in the utterance of his diction -
Creating world from word, a separate entity.
So tore out His heart, a form of male suttee.
As if God, immured in his pyre,
Saw the world fall in ashes from their fire.

An innocent from Heaven, yet a child
Such knowledge was discordant. She had riled
Against the wisdom of the patriarch
Now could find no satisfactory matriarch.
A law was broken, yet she learned to know
Love was possible still, it could flow
From her to him no matter what degree,
Leaving her palsied self on Calvary.
In the folkloric cabin, here first pictured,
She first received this love, unstrictured,
Freely given, as an afterthought
To each chiding, when child was over-wrought,
Who sought to win commerce from this ditch,
When love and sin, in contest grew, were rich.

Anomie, the river of our pain
Claps eyes on sunrise, never again
We'll witness like a child, a flower talk,
With the particles of sunlight take a walk –
In the golden kingdom where the mind can see
The majesty and beauty of *to be*

Now every child in our society
With TV experiences satiety,
And they are confused with images cheap,
On a constant mental bleep,
Putting stress on the mind's inner sanctum
Making archaic the holy benefactum
Everything to the child is history,
A tearing out of the heart of mystery.

Learning, of itself, brings much joy,
It doesn't matter which, girl or boy,
Can profit endlessly on life's mainstream
Actuality can be rendered into dream
The efflorescence of a captured thought
Can be reduced on paper to an X or Nought
Such is the magic of the elastic
Numbers, they are quite gymnastic,
So much so, they are masters of reality –
The world can be detonated to a t.
Reducing to rubble the cities of the plain,
Never from their ashes to rise again.
So what does God think, when we plot with glee
The application of his bright geometry?

THREE *our heroine, having time to think, unlike some of the people she knows, reflects on why not putting God first destroys our possibilities for living harmoniously in the world.*

So- postulate an order without God,
So - imagine love does not exist:
We now see the last century's rod,
Of unholy algebra and sex hieroglyph –

But believing in God is of the first order,
Then, loving the natural world which is His form
And this fusion makes we poets border
On ecstatic joy which is not the norm –
But those with the axiomatic right to shovel
Dirt in God's face, and not feel His reproof
Were an enigma to the heroine of this rhyming novel
Who set out to love, without bread or roof
Secure in the knowledge we were sinless,
In evil's hairy garden she was skinless.

To love God, and knowing of His care,
To see in His work – man and woman – a divinity
Is now considered an error truly rare,
If man is allied to benignity –
We are called to idolatry, a noxious thing
To worship the work, and not its maker
So Truth and Justice screech when they want to sing
Of Beauty, once more an unknown factor –
A man can, in a woman's beauty find
A nurturing spirit where his beauty heals
But without love, it becomes a bind
And the very place where her heart congeals
In making beauty chief in harmony
Receiving in return a lewd patrimony.

So love between two people is a scheme
Where now belongs destruction of a dream –
The beauty of her face gives him illusion
He can draw perfection from confusion –
Give shape to the world, richly endow

With meaning the bare here and now –
Yet, in her perished order is a chaos
Which to pursue and study, would pay us
In seeing in her broken form, a frown
Nature's supremacy will bring us down
In defeating death, and life, and strife –
All to be contemplated in a wife –
The basic fact of Nature's intransigence
Can be explored with some intelligence.

The tendency, however, is to ponder
Not on God's law being wrought asunder,
But in a small enclave, and dressed in lace
Smirk at the absurdity of the human race.
"You and I, my dear, have reached perfection –
The only thing for others is – rejection
Let them live by commerce and by trade
We'll get by without community aid
With a small income from my father's shares
And your teaching skills, we've honest wares –
Let others fulminate on the pedal bike
Let others fight about the right to strike
We have our car, our cocoon and our lid,
We're awfully glad we didn't have a kid."

But there is such love, such joy in being a mother
A woman knows it will be superseded by no other
Happiness, but with knowledge comes no boon –
Why give birth, when Death comes all too soon?
Uncaring Death lets fall the trapdoor's hinge
Forecloses life, as if an endless binge

In which the beauty of the world laid waste
Promises a ghastly fate of fates –
How could a child born out of love endure
The coldness of the earth, the air so pure
The mountains, seas and rivers all a ruin
Because God asked us to call the tune,
With greed and waste we sap His loving nerve
The demi-gods of earth will never serve.

There are exceptions who would live in truth
Their price is suffering, as the skin
Is stripped daily off by handsome youth,
Who hands out both, suffering, sin.
If she is bound up in the lie of history
Depression, then affliction, is her fare,
She may go inside the heart of mystery,
And find the Saviour there, to share
With him a crumb of grief or two,
And sip the vinegar on the spear,
See the foolishness of greed, woo
Instead the world-pain in a tear,
Better she be lonely, with God,
Than spend eternity, unclaimed, beneath a sod.

The terror of the ages, wrought in gold
Is now commodity, just bought and sold
No longer hard work and aspiration
Are paid for by sweat and perspiration
Satanic mills grind men, pulverise them
Unemployment, television hypnotise them,
Drugged dreams, like death and unreality

Lie at the heart a vampire of nullity.
Marriage of heart and minds no commonplace
We long for summer, with the snail's slow pace
Of perfection, before the rot sets in
Believing otherwise may be a sin
But what is sin, compared to love's fine graces
Hawked and whored for in the highest places?

FOUR – our heroine wonders if man and woman can truly love in the current climate of consumerism.

A man can love a woman, well, provided
She doesn't challenge anything at all
Where he might lose. So we have decided
First of all – we mustn't share the ball.
The man can now decided if he should
Show kindness or adventitious love,
While a woman had to do all she could
Just to be there with a man to shove.
So between theme, friction. And if she does
Decided to love beauty, then truth loses.
Therefore loving a man is getting on a bus
To falsehood. And women's ruses
Are the return fare. If love you must
Prepare to see your profile in the dust.

Ideas of love come before the feeling
Intrude themselves, a spotlight on the ceiling
Of our coveted desires. Much has been sung
Of trusting to love before we get our tongue.
The imminent shimmering of ardour
Is impossible to fake, and harder

157

Still it is, to yield to that first kiss
Without surrender. Tracts and tomes
Of women's liberation litter homes
An increment on bliss – here's one dame
Who ended up puzzled by the game,
If she said he was nice, why, he liked her,
And was kind to her, provided he was victor.

A measured joy friendship can pursue
After love's failed intimacy, ensue
An afterthought of closeness, on reflection
Between them now, a kind of genuflection –
True friendship is a bird, most rare,
Self interest often takes the lion's share
Of relationship. When one loves the other
As well as, or better than his mother –
Or even herself, when vanity goes to town
She sees in the mirror a face frown
So love has no place to set his seal
For good now, so what us real?
Now there's no part for the baby to play
He can't get through the plastic anyway.

Too often has the glint of promised rain
Spotted our sun-specks, and caused much pain
Once more the glimpse of burnished locks
Has cast our poets stranded on the rocks
Of faithless remorse. And love without belief
Is, of all phantoms, the worst thief.
The main and woman, icon of the plain
Now left far behind. And sex is the bane
They drink of until they die of thirst,

Murmuring to each other, who's the worst?
He, because he takes me for a synthesis
But not myself. She, because she is her thesis
Mocking at essential being. There's no ring,
Or baby, and they forget to sing.

If people could extend their love a little
They wouldn't treat their love as a skittle,
To be bowled at whenever, a hit and miss affair,
Unlike the world, which has tenure on the pair.
To love a neighbour is a tiring task
To love an enemy, more than one can ask
To treat another as if it were oneself,
To extend affection, protection, pelf
For no reason, just glory in the differ
Is asking much of life, the hefty biffer,
Who doles out disappointment, death and dirge
To hug yourself remains your only urge
To cosset in the name of fellow-feeling
A love which is a fly upon the ceiling.

A woman loved a man for what he does –
Boss, ideas guy, wage earner –
Inequality, they cried, and they choose
To march and sloganise, be bra-burner.
So the shoe's on the other foot, a man
Is a love object while the going is good –
His handsome face, his muscle, and his tan
Are assets now generally understood.
Does love and care shine from this Priapus?
Does woman feel cherished in her soul?
Men are now more likely to abuse us,

Distract us from our ever-widening goal
Equality has proved such an illusion
It has increased a hundred-fold, confusion.

A love between a woman, and a man,
Has in all ages, furnished poets with song
What happens now that woman starts to fan
Love's flickering flames with the wrong
Sex object? The man, once prerequisite
To the whole world, once possessed, was bliss
His attributes described as exquisite
What female poet has hand a hand in this?
Scarce one or two, and they have bid convention
Sit at their elbow while they penned their verse
Lest they give rise to fierce contention
That they were inappropriate or worse,
Being able to master the male art,
But unable to celebrate his part.

FIVE *– our heroine ponders further on the nature of human*
love – does it encourage self-interest, consumerism, and therefore
pollution?

If human love is only based on sex
Why is it such a feeling only wrecks
The state, the law, the constabulary
Attested for, time and again, in voluntary
Contributions to the free press. It seems
People are only really themselves in dreams,
And seldom think of any society
Save in terms of respectable sobriety.
So forget fellow-feeling, what's held in common
It's like the time Caesar crossed the Rubicon

And claimed all his. All now wish to own
Everything they see, or take a loan.
Sharing is now an idle vision
Best endured while watching television.

So annihilation is the structure of the whole
If we are given over to selfish goal,
Conquest, conspiracy, exploitation
Murder, pillage, and infiltration.
The past excesses of extinct society
Were bent with its own satiety -
What's left but conquering neighbour's lands
Intimidation, weapons, not loving bands,
No wholesome hearts to expand without friction
Trying to prove that war is just a fiction.
Not so at all. Instead we have the spectacle
Of warring nations, and peace lovers ramshackle.
Swords into ploughshares! What optimism.
Did someone say light breaks up in a prism?

To survive, we must expand the caring zone,
Embrace others we would not call our own.
When we rush to buy a motor car
Remember, though we travel very far
We leave unfriendly fumes, pillage the earth
For which future generations will feel dearth.
The honking snakes of traffic in a city
For perambulating babies have no pity,
The layer of ozone in the stratosphere
Is diminishing for sure, year by year,
Hamburgers are eating into forests
Acid rain is making stone quite porous

The bombs are piling up – while a homily
Tells us all that is important is our family.

Appeasing the voracious household god
Is simply now a matter of the right wad
Of notes. The world may yet turn desert
If unhappy couples continue to subvert
Nature, and her wise house-keeping way.
Future generations will have to pay –
Unless, of course, someone drops the bomb
And the world itself become an ashen tomb!
God spare us, but 'twould perplex you,
Pain, terrorise, affright and vex you –
But something in our purpose is germane
To this most overwhelming side-track: the main
Thrust of my argument is why people
Feel love is only congruent 'neath a steeple.

The kernel of the matter is what people feel
    -   Romantic Love – is self and unreal.
Let those who wish to exploit, do so.
Do they deserve their riches? Rousseau
Gave us a common humanity outside the state,
But it's enough for me that I tolerate my mate
And reign supreme in my own front room,
It has no view, save the TV, and the womb.
And then when we build our air-raid shelter
We'll have it so when we run helter-skelter
And the sirens sounding, there'll be a few
Left of us, perhaps just me and you.
So therefore, the idea of man and wife,

Somehow always ends up in strife.

So science is the genius for our age,
It governs life at every stage
From neonatology to the mortician's skill,
Reproduction, from sterility to the pill.
Two-headed monkeys, smoking dogs, and worse
Obscenities which wouldn't decorate a verse,
Pets with eyes burning with chemicals
Just to show us what brand of syrup kills
Rats climbing on endless treadmills,
To the desired end we should understand all ills.
Science has made babies in test-tubes,
And with mammeoplasty can construct new boobs,
Science has made these bombs, without God's adduction
To bring about his gorgeous world's destruction.

The good fairy at birth, was in no hurry,
First time to learn language, less a worry,
Communication was our raison d'etre
Truth the by-product, our onlie beggeter.
Yet when people let science go to their heads
They put everyone in different beds -
A definition to shred common humanity
Separating us and them, you and me.
Discrimination is our culture's crown
Best when worn upside down.
To celebrate diversity should be our aim,
Not sacrificing people to the game
Of science, but with our best love hurled
To welcome each child into the world.

It is only in this age we seek to ask
If the nature of our love is worth the task
Why, in the empty grillroom of the heart,
We analyse, dissect a lover's part.
Our essence is a physical thrill
Which can be regulated by a pill.
Love's dream upon the pillow of the night
Is torn apart by analysis. The right
Of others is tabled in the law,
Our recourse when love fails. The raw
Incarnate being of spirit's good
Is questioned in our structure of the good.
The storied wonder of a pair of eyes
Can be ourselves, in alter ego guise.

It's hard for such matter to see above the ground,
The nosedive of the spirit often found,
And traced in the annals of the monks, whose day
Is structured around canticle and lay
Putting body pleasure on the lowest level
A provenance belonging to the devil.
Love is elevation to our Godly nature
Growing in essence from our moral stature,
Not physical display. It reached its height
The milli-second before the serpent urged the bite,
And showed in poisoned speech just what he was,
A perversion of true love and its laws,
Renunciation then became the very acme,
The height of love was caring for your enemy.

God made man and woman in His image,
Vaunting our peerage in the heavenly lineage,
Adam, progenitor of the human race,
Had longed to behold a loving face,
The lineaments of which utmost ecstasy
Was translated, in affliction, to a tree,
So men and women then refused expectation
Of being god-like through obedience, a dedication
To one full transcript of authority,
In which evil in good found no sanctuary,
So when the shroud of mortality began to tear,
Their impulse was to don clothes, and to wear,
The invisible cloth that had bound them to their duty,
Making palpable their curiosity, waking their beauty.

Response is more than half-a-lover's due,
If that love can be linked with expectation,
And if that response is laced with woman's rue,
What's left is what's bestowed on the nation
Not a necessary fiction to lend society
The dream that love exists, that love is all,
No matter wars, or blood-propriety
Truth can't be silenced, it's a call.
So, in the home, the world, there's a kind of friction
Because imagination often makes for fiction,
If the love man has for woman is just a part,
There cannot be peace within the heart
To write in her prayer-book, be transistor
Not add to lies they have told your sister.

Her sacrifice to truth was dearly paid

Would she have been better off a maid?
Not dallied, having spent her honey-pot,
On a careless rapture decency forgot.
His first kiss sealed her in the prison
Of her fancied dreams – where she could listen
Now to the rolling thunder of the skies,
Bereft, beleaguered, and filled with tawdry lies
Humbug, man's truth, philosophy in jest,
Who believes in the eternal quest?
Discounting God, and loveliness, and truth,
In the proverbial wasted youth,
A woman who loved this man became false
To herself by the end of the waltz.

But if to find love, we must consult authority,
Find there written the story of the human race,
How do we know that it isn't just a story,
Designed to keep us ignorant when face to face,
Feeling a powerful attraction for each other,
Do we care if it's written in the law,
When we don't need law to love our mother,
Or you can't make someone love you with the raw
Emotion that we feel when we're repulsed,
Or the way we just hate someone on sight,
Does the law answer to a pulse?
Or does it take our measurements at night.
Talking of duty is all very well,
But we're not Pavlov's dogs responding to a bell.

How can we love when we don't know who it is
Telling us how to act in life,
Do we allow them to ration out our bliss,

166

Or designate who should be a wife,
But there are times that feeling's such a jumble
I don't know if I hate and love at once,
Does God exist just to make me humble,
To feel after all my learning, I'm just a dunce?
All I know, when I hand you to His care
I trust the universe, it seems to sing,
The order in it is like a beautiful prayer,
As if an angel had given me a wing,
Truth is there's no way such an order could exist
Without an artist, skilled in love, and kissed.

SEVEN – *our heroine wonders, as she feels the problems
bringing a child into a world full of problems, if Art can heal us?*

What's art, but love's enduring rapt caress,
Of mind, and heart, unsullied by duress,
Nor bought and sold, but spirit unenslaved,
By hint of conquest, history's architrave.
Sometimes, blood rushes to the loved one's cheek
At the wantonness by which the poets seek
Eternity in the coil of golden hair
An anodyne like alabaster, or ointment rare –
To wrap in shrouds the heart's secret treasure
To live as long as Pharaoh, and be measure
Of the deep intimacy of two souls' union
Transcendent flesh, and spirit in communion.
The beloved's face can be mask or map,
A divine spring where goodness is on tap.

But often twenty years must run its course,
Before our story can begin to force
Apart conjunction, and time. Coincidence
Woven with the heart's desire, a dissidence
Because sometimes two don't meet. Mask
And distraction to furnish a crack. Ask
A woman, man or child for meaning,
Into our apocalyptic century, leaning
Heavily on art for interpretation
Of the pain and fury of their station,
Where God is banished, yet where gods remain,
To haunt our souls with beauty, a domain
In which our love and work seeks inspiration
In the aetiolated sociology of our nation.

History is the affluent confusion
Of victorious enemies in collusion
What's registered important has no bearing
On who's done the loving and the caring,
Who built the house, often fails to mention
The carpenter and mason in dissension
The bricklayers, plumbers and all the rest,
Leave unmarked testimony to their quest
For perfection and craft in honest toil –
Too soon forgotten, in the hurried spoil.
Likewise, a victor soon forgets what's banished,
The homes, he's wrecked, and the hearts he's
vanquished.
The conqueror only admitting a version of the story
When he is cast in praise and sung in glory.

The silence from the public has been deafening

168

Inside the minds of tiny tots, are beaming
Hopeless generations of a tired world,
The brickbats and insults once were hurled
From the craggy depths of depravity,
To defy the hallowed pull of gravity,
Now stand, still, in piled-up arsenals
Pledging the utmost necrophilia, the calls
Of infant babes for peace to live among us,
To unlearn our conflicts. . Who would bung us
Into the ash-pit of history, a final testament
To humanity, 'intrinsic worthless excrement',
So a little child contemplates suicide,
Seeing on TV the race's glorious fratricide.

The wound in us, has been called Original Sin,
It drives the heart, makes it conscript in
The soul's stumbling, ailing, healing,
Tying the balloon of fancy to the ceiling,
Witness of the spirit's searching liberty,
Coming unstuck on the outskirts of sobriety.
To taxi in the grief of freedom spent.,
And leave a lasting, deathless, monument
To millions who died in war, because of a strife
When death seemed preferable to life.
The fact is, mankind's being prone to error
Has achieved an anguished, sophisticated terror,
Which has made our true reality a sadness
As we contemplate our final madness.

Peace lies within us, like a rainbow.
And loves to give warring hearts a show
Away from the lusted caravans of the past

Where bloodied bodies heaped, for centuries cast
One on another in a burning grill,
Furnishing devils with a secret thrill.
Yet way above this fiery conflagration
Flies a dove, whose wing beat in exaltation
In a summer house intended for all seasons,
A child's caravan trailing all the reasons
We should love one another until we die,
So living in the majestic heaven's sky,
- Justice, Rapture, Joy and Intelligence,
No more broken hearts which spell intransigence.

Each child is a beginning, that's for sure,
There's endless possibility with each birth,
Free from hunger and thirst, who could ask for more,
And happiness maybe on our lovely earth.
If peace comes, and they put away the bombs,
I'll be thankful I had my child to love
From Nature, the seas, and CD Roms,
My heart will be bursting to prove
That nothing will destroy my love of good,
That nothing will break my heart again,
This child is hope for all I've ever been,
The best I have seen in women and men,
When I'm pushing him into the world, I'll say a prayer,
That God will enfold us in His care.

Faustina in Sestinae

*Winner of the Scottish Open International Poetry
Competition, Epic, 2004*

ONE

A young girl brought up as innocent
Has one desire, the desire to be loved
She falls in love with a handsome man
But he fears her love and he rejects
Her aspirations and her finitude
Material she is but built for the spirit

For human kind is founded on the spirit
And human nature essentially innocent
Except for the hard degree of finitude
And the need from birth to be loved
Which prophesies misdeeds for the rejected
All depend for acceptance on the man

If he refuses the gift, a strumpet man
For handsome he may be of body and of spirit
She is like a queen by kingdom rejected
For such was she a queen of the innocent
For she badly needs to be loved
And this for her is dismal finitude.

And worse than that a darkening finitude
In the shape of a particularly handsome man
He has forgotten her wish to be loved
But strives as one demented for her spirit
That is at once lovely and innocent
In a supreme atavism she is his rejected

His incarnate idealised and idolised rejected
That shapes for ever her sense of finitude

She is at once forever the innocent
Taken on a nasty jolting ride by a man
Who demeans her by offering a paltry spirit
And who stays sublime because so loved

And lives in the world of gods because he's loved
And not in the world of mortals rejected
In body and inconsequence the lack of spirit
Which is now a most demeaning finitude
A post-lapsarian state of man
Which cannot imagine once all were innocent

Being rejected increases finitude
Being loved makes a saint of a man
Which revives the spirit of the innocent.

TWO

Being young does not avoid the unreal
Reality of relationships. To death we hasten
In a medley charismatic of a sect
Belonging to no one to ourselves we deaden
The unripe exegesis of our seconding coming
Towards the unbecoming toward of a sign

Hoping against hope we will find a sign
Signalling madly that love is so unreal
Yet real as the first coming
Of a blade of grass into the world to hasten
The nurturing of things not yet undeaden
In the belief that life is the universal sect

And not just a closed and scientific sect
Waiting to be translated into a sign
Whose ultimate withholding power is to deaden
Meaning until it is elided in the unreal
At whose door the prophet will hasten
To warn the world of the truth's coming

And we shall know it in the moment of coming
And we shall tear up sect by sect
Any confidence trick conceived to hasten
The passing of a lie and of a sign
For all lie and confection is unreal
Embracing the absent truth to deaden

Our hearts our minds our temples deaden
With congealed fact the limbo of our coming
To terms with the real or unreal
And in the absence of a fictive sect
Look for a final and absolute sign
So when we embrace love we can hasten

To the womb-tomb matrix, hasten
Like the hound of heaven whose teeth deaden
On the simulacra contusions of a sign
Around the truth real as the coming
Of anything which makes love a sect
And dethrones the King of the unreal

A will to deaden the ghostly coming
A wish to hasten the lovers' sect
In a longed-for sign that is not unreal.

THREE

Mainly she wanted to be wanted
Unhappy since zero was her target
She acted with longing that was purely wanton
Her body sang with broken tunes in her head
Above all, she desired above desire
A desire that eluded its own secret

The hole in her soul was a secret
To disguise she wanted to be wanted
She became her own dark desire
Eternal friendship was her target
Co-existent with the longing in her head
Her whole existence became entirely wanton

A love for desire is purely wanton
Especially desire that is so secret
Disguised as friendship only in her head
Her heart did not admit it was not wanted
So the false friendship was the target
In the real masquerade of desire

Desire all consuming in desire
But for an ugly man it was so wanton
Desire for her was an easy target
Since desire for him was an open secret
That's what comes of wanting to be wanted
It makes passionless pain in the head

And makes grievous grief in the head
Since the destination of all desire

Is to turn the unwanted into the wanted
And makes of sincere women a very wanton
This cannot be called a class of secret
Since it is true lovers' only target

To make of life and love no target
But aimless in compassion like a head
Which enfolds the mystery's living secret
When desire becomes only desire
And true feeling is never wanton
But knows the joy of being truly wanted

So breaks a head with fulfilled desire
A target reached a peaceful wanton
A secret heart of being wanted.

FOUR

He wasn't beautiful but he aspired to beauty
He wasn't clever but he was smart with people
He read enough to quote the literati
Stun with an apt quotation from his head
He liked her body and for this her soul
Was his for he had vowed never to part

She was beautiful and desired never to part
Particularly from contemplation of her own beauty
So determined envisaged a bartered soul
Which wasn't good for explaining to people
Where one was at turning the head
Of the attendant scribbling literati

But soon they were receding literati
For they had been only playing a part
And the intoxication of lust went to their head
Like her they were drawn to active beauty
But you know how it is with people
Eventually they hope to capture the soul

And then sit around, defining, explaining soul
Soul had been written off by the literati
So when they hear of progress of people
They say their soul will never take part
That the eternal quality of beauty
Dances like angels on the material pinhead

Lust makes love its celebrant, a head
Severed on the dancing of the soul
Which wants to remain quiet before beauty
This is no good to the literati
Who want more than anything to play a part
Building bridges between themselves and the people

For we are living in an age when rule of the people
It's not the heart that counts but the head
If severed now, they are for centuries apart
Then who has freedom to speak of the soul
But the newspaper columns and the literati
And they don't inspire or create much beauty

He gains a head, she's chanced her soul
The song of the people echoes the literati
Never to part with, never to stay with beauty.

FIVE

Being the personification of an ideal
A woman has half a chance of being real
Who vaunts her for her feminine quality
Ends up by despising her for her vanity
A thought that is rare can seem affectation
When considered beside waning physical attraction

But a lonely thought can be an attraction
To a spiralling spirit starving in the ideal
For who can believe in affectation
Besides the hunger to feel real
Even sincerity can be thought vanity
When there is no other quality

Surely all that matters is quality
The gut response to a high attraction
Which has very little to do with vanity
The surging clarity of an ideal
Which has less chance of being real
Married to style it seems an affectation

There are some who prove all is affectation
Even in the discovery of pure quality
They fail to find the unreal and the real
Uplifted by the dualistic attraction
And sustained by the nobly held ideal
Heads close like flowers in full vanity

As the preacher saith, all is vanity
And these tousled heads of puzzled affectation

Put a clear glass before the ideal
One luminous moment of quality
Which has such a powerful attraction
One begins to wonder what is real

And the more substantial claim, the real
Takes over the numinous insight
And clarity has its own attraction
Hoping it will not seem an affectation
But the one indispensable quality
Is the need for the beauty of the ideal

Such is vanity, an affectation
Such is the real, it has quality
Such is the ideal, it has attraction.

SIX

Of all the schemes that seemed the most utopian
Here was the new man made by the machine
His songs would be guttural and grunting monotonously
And his insights the validity of utilitarianism
With the right class system he would be happy
He would be happy to work for the state

Not of unfulfilled longings but the daily bread state
Dry and dusty and greyly utopian
At such a table she could not be happy
Such a table had been made by a machine
Such was the lacklustre world of utilitarianism
Before long she was singing monotonously

A mouth groaning and singing monotonously
May have suited the purpose of the state
In their abject worship of utilitarianism
The dusty imagination in this low utopia
When man thinks like a machine
His soul becomes blue and unhappy

The blues are born to make the unhappy happy
But far from replicating monotonously
They couldn't find the full scale of the music machine
Which needless to say didn't please the state
Utility, not beauty is the message utopian
Which as we all know is undeniably utilitarian

A poet could tell you that the utilitarian
Lacks vision, beauty or what can make you happy
Which is a leap to the notion of utopian
A life lead with utilities is a life led monotonously
Which is the main achievement of the state
Which makes the human being into a machine

Is man's happiness compatible with the machine
Do we have to say goodbye to utilitarianism
That would put us in another state
In pure being when we could be happy
And play with machines but not monotonously
To leave them out altogether would not be truly utopian

A form of utilitarianism is to manufacture being happy
Use the machine, but not live monotonously
Long live the state, long live utopia.

SEVEN

Suppose she thought there was a combination
A sort of positive mixed-up mode
Where the proletarian could have spiritual
Appetites for poetry and the good
Where one could have decent ambition
For art and beauty which are eternal

Could they be cast in love which is eternal
For love and hate are no combination
And love is often stifled by ambition
And becomes a habit, an outdated mode
Who is to know what is for the good
When all leads ultimately to the spiritual

She chose a lover who was a little spiritual
A flink flecked core of an eye eternal
Which showed he leaned somewhat to the good
But what exactly was his combination
Remains a mystery in the cuckoo's mode
He had earthy roots and he had ambition

In fact he had quite a lot of ambition
And not a lot of it was spiritual
And he affected a belief, a mode
That called her to be his new friend eternal
Promised to love her in any combination
Promised fidelity to beauty and the good

But mostly to himself which was the main good
To be loved for herself was all her ambition

To be desired her only combination
And that was more physical than spiritual
And what was physical must become eternal
Lust in action being the only mode

Expense of spirit being the lesson mode
To lose oneself and sight of the good
So cheating oneself of what is eternal
Promises on flesh are perverse ambition
To deify the ordinary, make it spiritual
Flesh and spirit a fatal combination

To be good may lack ambition
A mode of being only spiritual
Everything eternal, in endless combination.

EIGHT

Who will know the joy of the beloved
Fit to transfer to a wordy kingdom
Of flesh to celebrate the arcane delight
Of voyagers' footsteps in the mesh of flesh
When friendship was all that was asked
And counterfeit reality a political dream

And dream of a dream, objective dream
We finger thoughts of the beloved
When he through nightmare was asked
To mimic the lover's kingdom
In a free exchange of flesh for flesh
That still yielded the odd delight

But only the shadow of delight
Could be token lust for a real dream
As if the mind were built on flesh
Spirit and matter at one in the beloved
Yet loved not in desire's kingdom
When friendship was all that was asked

And being friendship. no one was asked
Who would rob an angel's eye of delight
Swap the sores of a dispossessed kingdom
And ransom honour in a real dream
Put away all thoughts of the beloved
As if the beloved was merely of flesh

Yet dreaming dreams of heavenly flesh
Much more than friendship often was asked
To abandon for ever all hope of the beloved
In whose presence is eternal delight
This was an impossible dream
Of reality admitted to the lovers' kingdom

For there is no doubt love is a kingdom
Friendship a democracy abdicating the flesh
But there is no lie in this awakening dream
When all thoughts of friendship asked
To be put away for pure delight
Of spirit in the arms of the beloved

So, of flesh, a question not asked
Yet hoped for is a kingdom of delight
Again, again we dream of the beloved.

NINE

In the third revolution there was a shedding
Not of blood, but of ideas of blood
That meant an interruption of birth
Being constantly postponed for want of good
A still birth frozen moment of endless becoming
Nothing moved forward, it was endless flux

And flux on dancing gyrating flux
Photographs captured the moment of shedding
Into the future that was an endless becoming
Blood seems less real than red blood
And less real seemed the idea of good
The substantive good had a still birth

Not still, but violent end to birth
A lifeless bringing forth in endless flux
All that being necessary a sense of good
But necessary in its ultimate shedding
Of trust and honour linked with blood
In order to make a real becoming

Force, ordain or grant becoming
As becoming as the generation of birth
Accompanied as in real life with blood
But this was real even in the flux
Right and wrong parted and were shedding
Tears at the separation of evil and good

The continuous final achievement of good
That would allow celestial becoming

A glorious constant renewal shedding
Departure and farewells greeting birth
In the heart's secret mansions of flux
As the true moment between spirit and blood

Inspirit life fountain of crystal blood
Ruby jewel and diamond of the good
Unseen in the crowd's hurrying flux
And given to them in their becoming
As long as they do not forsake birth
In their long-for osmosis, of human shedding

The tree of good, the fruit for becoming
Without blood, there can be no birth
Without water's flux, no carnal shedding.

TEN

The first invasion is the thud of word
In the name of God killing has begun
The kingdom on earth must beget death
Innocence murdered by the women's ministry
That thinks itself liberated into life
A life and death ordained by the patriarchy

For women must fit into the patriarchy
In the beginning was the male word
Inspiriting matter it begot life
And from man, not woman, was life begun
Then men took over the ministry
At the centre power leading to death

And for centuries they had a love of death
Death was inseparable from the patriarchy
And death, not life, became the ministry
Such was the power of the word
And since women's liberation has begun
Women have power over death and life

And choosing power, chose death over life
Death of the unborn, most horrible face of death
Just after the seed and egg have begun
New life not accepted by the patriarchy
So life is again a matter for the word
Choose choice is the name of the new ministry

And choosing death is an evil ministry
Knowledge of the price paid for life
Knowledge to know more beyond the word
To seek, to suck out, to meet death
Carnal knowledge and elemental patriarchy
Is the way through which perdition has begun

For power and knowledge in ruination has begun
And power and knowledge are the women's ministry
That makes them indistinguishable from the patriarchy
Ends in a waver, a woman for an infant's life
For one or the other, one must choose death
For in the beginning is life, made the word

Women's ministry should stand for life
What is begun must not abort in death
Nor return to the patriarchy, but return to the word.

ELEVEN

Who reads this book shall have first refusal
On the offer of an eternal friendship
What women whose soul is lost to marriage
Cannot but turn to bartering hope
In the unforeseen joy of exchange
A feast of books in lieu of a body

For law has decreed she was materialist body
For this she has fully signed her refusal
To be thought fit for any kind of exchange
All that was left was eternal friendship
In the pit of despair it was a black hope
In the tawdry desecration of a marriage

For she was property, gained same in marriage
What was deemed worthy was her peerless body
Which gave her youth quite a false hope
Of postponing age, a life-long refusal
To be on terms other than eternal friendship
Was the only possible kind of exchange

And made possible through this exchange, exchange
Her life a thing then, through a false marriage
All that was left was eternal friendship
In which she viewed herself a lender of her body
And given once, there was no refusal,
For such refusal would have given up hope

And what is worse in life than a false hope
Better the ancient wisdom of exchange

Spirit for matter would bring no refusal
In such a way escape from the tainted marriage
No money in question for her lovely body
Under the guise of eternal friendship

And such was the notion of eternal friendship
That it knocked over the effigy of hope
And left her sprawling like a doll body
A spirit for matter is no fair exchange
And lust is a cowboy who scoffs at marriage
Giving texture and touch to her refusal

And who's to hope for a free exchange
Eternal friendship a parody of marriage
All for a body yea-saying its refusal.

TWELVE

The great temptation is desiring heaven on earth
For that creates monolith in the people
Intrude, invade, insult their private feelings
Holding them as illicit trash
Appoint guardians of the public morality
Great wet nurses who bond the will

And in that structured anomie kill will
Those who rule to bring heaven on earth
Invade the soul and tie up with morality
The exuberance of a spirit of a people
So they exhale and say it's plain trash
And has nothing to do with our feelings

189

And what have we indeed besides our feelings
Only and violated held-down restrained will
Only the tamed effulgence that is called trash
By the bituminous glow of a night watchman on earth
Open to the night we feel the dance of the people
Shift from one foot to another at the mention of morality

For we cannot legally express our morality
Bringing heaven to earth, and then dampen feeling!
Such is the sawdust fed to the people
Who everyday through an act of betrayal, the will
Is languidly hurt in the moist globe earth
Which has been reduced by history to trash

Consumer durables, artefacts of trash
You yet trumpet your transient morality
The one log on earth is ownership
Is this not the most flatulent of feelings
And yet how it nourishes, upbraids the will
Which resides in despots governing the people

So what hope is there for the spirit of people
Believe and do not consign to the trash
Belief in the future, belief in the will
For there is only one morality
We must live and love with our true feelings
Which will create a future on earth

So out with trash, and in with morality
Great people have good feelings
At last the will for heaven and earth.

Selected Earlier Poems

From: The Broken Pledge (1985)
THE IDLE ROAD (a *rondeau redouble*)
Quelled in the spirit are my plans and schemes
And malediction on my proper loss;
Fled from the battle all my rebel dreams,
Chimerical ghosts my wayward path now cross,

And with their tinny laughter pain emboss
At cunning failure's retrograding beams,
The centre of my turmoil is Eros,
Quelled in the spirit are my plans and schemes

Consigned to paper, where they lie in reams
To be consumed in flames in which I toss,
The sportive tendrils with which my fancy teems,
And malediction on my proper loss.

When inaction produces such a dross,
Being is what does, and not what seems –
Meretricious art now rewards my doss,
Fled from the battle all my rebel dreams.

No reaping to be done, and what I deem
Worthy would quite dement a boss.
A single gleaner, I scorned all teams,
Chimerical ghosts my wayward path now cross.

The proverb's true, I gather little moss.
There, the super-ego seeds in gleams,
Awake, my lazy heart, to other themes,
And tomorrow, I will flee this house of joss...
Quelled in the spirit...

THE BOOK OF RIGHTS

Your eyes are many pages
Of a dictionary I have lost –
Star-crossed, and down-wards shine
Cutting bright gems on my inward floor,
Your face, in the mask of its ecstasy,
Is love (in relief)
I feel the night-wood thistle of your cheek.
For I have followed you,
My heart's impurity,
Were symbiotic glances
Have sent me into trances,
In front of Government buildings,
Under the stares of policemen,
I tugged at your woollen sleeve
And only found your badge of office,
Where a red banner played hawser to my wing.
If I have lost
The exotic life of my verbless youth,
I recover it now,
In the papyrus of your skin,
With its inkblots,
The scars, the ideallic wars,
That were the mill, the treadle, the coin,
And I would have loved you all this time,
If only I believed in your strange words.
Words can make,
Paper tigers can destroy,
A body of ontological kinaesthesia*
Is not a toy.
*book

BEFORE I WAS MARRIED

Let us create a God of love,
As the stars circle our heads,
Orion still has his cuirass of light
In the icy wastes of white dwarves' night
A million stars are burning bright

You are no phoenix, as you stir
Among the ashes of the dream,
You are no spark to be a flame
No heavy possibility –

Let me translate your state
Of unaffected hope,
In such a way as may grieve you,
Who makes satins out of the useless
And still think sport is beautiful –
What makes you survive in an age of reproductions?

As you live in your lonely grange,
No bard will elevate your name,
No hint of paint like acetate
Will make you regenerate,
No silk, nor chiffoned sleeves beguile
The hardened exegesis of your tainted eye,
Nor beauty too real, like Absalom's fair hair,
Betray you.

Still, I'll not rest till I discover
Your song that lies like a chrysalis
Along the glimmer of your throat –

That sad soul of yours, astray,
Affects no inclination to betray
The last wish of mine

That you be more prolific than a candleabra
Sweeter than purple fuchsia,
Creating illumination.

Striding along in any city,
We have a common situation,
The tired and restless friction of my soul
Will not bear interruption,
While your fingers tap,
Cast shadows on my mind,
Point to reason as a
Necessary good.

"We live in silence."
"No, we live between the silences."

THE FAIR-HAIRED BOY

It was with ransom I was born,
And hungered in a molten way,
And ran the thousand wonderfalls
Of sight and hearing at their play.

I crossed the deep in silent bliss
And in my chariot to the moon,
I sang upon the edge of night,
And hit the galaxy in tune.

So sweetly heard the melody
That I became the singer's ploy,
There was sweet mending to be done,
I turned into a golden boy.

So beautiful, my face is fair,
My eyes rim sunlight by the hour,
My twin-starred, gentle, iron soul,
Is honey in my mother's bower.

THE BROKEN PLEDGE

Was knowing you the grace of this, my heart,
Which became a concubine of art,
Embroidered as our first acquaintance, brief.
I knew you then, or else had I as life,
Made such study of your charms and airs,
Counted individual your hairs,
Sized up your moral worth, and balanced all,
The final reckoning, assets in a squall.

While the analytic with its knife
Prunes the verge of every loving eye,
Why marry who will dwindle into wife?
When across the sky at dawn, Selene's I.
I leave the world to absence, and to grief,
Because thought chewed upon my ivory leaf,
Panted after gods consumed in fire
And made of mortal love and hope – a pyre.

Can I, in dumb and empty grief, confine
Your coffin in this seaward slope of lime?
The green sward will grow high, and thick, and strong –
The years of mourning marrying, too long;
And yet such rampant growth across your grave,
With many a shivering shock, a soul could save.
I am guilty as charged, reason for your strife,
I never, ever loved you as a wife.

Love locked its doors on me, its laws defied –
For want of willingness, you lost me, your side,
Hope gone, I spin a web to last an age,

Which glimmers like a tear upon the page.

The page is written, and the love still lives,
Although no love from you my heart receives
Your body waits, before the clayey ground,
While like a ring, I turn our life around.

If, to love freedom, I did let you go,
Before your twinning eyes had made it night,
Before your hidden loveliness was bought,
And twined to my illusory right,
Before your face ranged like a talented spy
Tenured as the sceptre of my eye,
Before the dauphin hopes of this, my song,
Were measured by the tailor, and the thong –
So go, my love, for I will see you more
Lovely afar, and by this light
I swear my freedom makes your bondage bite.

If, in my rapt despair of healing words,
Your windless eye seeks in me, a crown,
I'll hang it upon my breath, like a two-edged sword,
To lead me to the gallows, life done down.
If sacrifice to truth I have to make,
I'll dye it with a rending of my hair,
A parting of my eye to give you joy,
Before I pull the curtain on my ploy.

But, no such perjured whim I'll need to limn,
Your gracious bow of truth is born of limb,
Too fine for art, too lovely to be lie,
Too beautiful, in truth, you do not die:

But live forever in that golden dawn
When magic filled the heart of everyone,
Dissection led only to the grave,
Its spirit answers back, a wave upon a wave.

Were I too moved to tell the lightening way,
Your hands and shoulders risk the arc of day
Ranging all choristers with the dying throng,
Were I too cold, too far, to touch the light
In which your face moves, and my eyes shut tight
To cancel out with beauty, every wrong.
Were I too deaf t hear the tumbrel chant
Each resonance of your coveyed throat filters,
Were I too dumb to say I love you much,
I'd say it still, who can only blossoms vouch.

If, solely and only, you were all my love –
All the thick-tufted forest, and the coloured sea,
The wind that shakes the barley in the lea,
And the anti-matter whorl which no eye can see.
Then the poetry of reflection would be your garden,
In a red rose refracted in the gyre,
But not annihilated by our fire,
So if skies, and souls, by freedom aren't devoured,
I trust that by this faith, a hope is endowered.

Were pity to myself a leasing love,
I'd have it dressed in languor, so to prove,
I didn't care, a jot, or an iota, for you,
Disguise by fulsome pride my wicked rue,
But loving you gives hoping for an age,
Another day, you'll walk upon my stage.

I'll challenge you to ask if feeling's all,
When I have pinned your armour to the wall.

The future to a woman has no pretence,
At some point, she will sacrifice to sense.
When I had hope written high above the door,
My love for you was dead, it was no more.
So for this death of love, I'll make a wreath,
A thing to mourn my life and love, in death,
And coffin it in words, a useless reel,
A wattle box of rhyme, and thought, in streel,
Around it I will bind your lock of hair,
To keep our love alive for evermore.

If, at the bridge-end's day of winter comes
A riding Prince, with apples in his mouth,
Would I then listen to an auguring bird,
Would *Rosa Mystica* flourish in a drought?
Now afternoon's the only harking twang,
In a church, where cressets flutter out,
And a young man dies, a mandrake, while a scream
Belies the vapourless stillness of his breath,
Where once the stopping mirror regards void,
And pinches windfalls from his silver throat.

THE ZOO AND THE SEA

The gesture is the shape of flame
Which tells how sacred is a name.

The Grail is lost, and yet we keep
Making comparisons, and cheap.

Follow monkeys in cages, where amused
They scan the weekend solitudes.

A grid necessary, but fractious,
Come, poet, be friend, and tax us.

At least we here have no pretence
Amenable to common sense,

We set our flag above the door
Gouge wide the existential sore.

We are all one species, so stay on
Here's an ill-fitting paradigm for everyone.

Recognise what is good and true,
Leave faith, all will follow you.

And wallow blindly in the sand
For fate to hold, and lend a hand.

Just say that mire reflects a star

- the essence of what people are,

And lying, they can easily fake
The watershed of their own make.

Live in inaction, like the clam
Devour the air, and eat "I am".

Be sunk in strange nobility
Like lobster pots in a blood red sea.

The teeth advent the coming rage,
Cry, and tear up every page.

History is made by agreed omission
Only the sea is true to its mission

We sit here, watching its vindication
As it is pumped full of radiation.

THE RAFT

From temples hiding from his wrath,
Where fool and Pharisee sit in sackcloth,
From places where the Holy Writ is banked
My raft set out to sea – one faithful plank.

The discourse on love was a novelty, so stated
The whinge of servility in the highly fated
The constant profanity in public places
Seen as a blemish on the ancient graces

"No Blame", at the conference on Recidivism,
Pungent satire to expel the scroll's witticism,
Whispering behind hands, convent girl on parole
Finds herself word-perfect on the soul.

It must be love, for I have still my heart,
It beats in me, that is God's balanced part
Every truth makes the mind effective
Every thought is the action's corrective;

Yet arms and munitions are hidden under rants
To make dismemberment speak, to lance
With foetid spear the halo of identity
And obfuscate the human destiny

But He, who drove the waves beneath the firmament,
Can speak in divers tongues, a promise meant:
He, who can see the rot the land has set you,
Was torn in anguish to perfect you.
Grasp hope, the raft of a new season –

Render unto joy the affliction of your reason;
Believe a friend, who loves you more than He?
Is all the answer finding God has victory?

So hope, listen, is a word sent to the heart,
A loving eye, yet which is not upstart:
From the garb of selfhood, which imprisons,
From the ruin of churches, which is schisms,

From the abuse of freedom, which is tyranny –
Deliver us, said the detritus of the faithful sea,
From the usurper's investment in the Evening Star
Save us, cried the man who would not cull the Morning
Glory's hour.

DEAD MAN'S FINGERS

No compass, lodestar, nor muted caulborn child,
Could have taken away our chancery
So much, nor in the abandoned wild
Of Seafarers' destinies, scrawled this history

On faces chiselled by the sea, to doom
Of blood and breath. And sea thrift, a waste
Of what the verb *to be* means. Boom
Of nefarious husbandry, they will reap

From the spendthrift sea a wreck of haggards,
Scratch on the sand a white, deformed defeat,
And the advertising in the paper, braggarts
That only what is visible is meat

For enterprise, where maiden wombs will shape
Children born to die of master rape.

THE SHIP OF STATE

The ship of state, she was a frozen image
Grown out of bloodshed, murder, adage.
Inward-gazing brought her short of hysteria,
And banished her writers to outer Siberia,

Hocked soul, spirit, mind for foreign exchange,
Swallowed ideas, till they grew a mange,
Advertisement, sugar stick of seduction
Ground her on the rock of destruction.

The shores polluted, the rivers stinking, rotten
Show how our less-than-modern state was begotten,
The air is full of fumes from motor cars,
With smoke, from the heating up of little Czars.

The sea, cogitates, warning starfish,
To assume the shape of anguish.

NEREID
(For Sheila and Val Iremonger, and their family)

There is a place I'm sure to find my song
Although it echo when the night winds blow
And the harbour fill with tambourines of woe,
When embittered sailors rowing hard and slow
Tell of how time has made the story long
And in so doing, lost its maiden tongue
Yet there's a place where death won't sound his gong.

There is a place I know a barren reed
Moons in the river, like a frozen note,
Its delicate calligraphy afloat
To bear the honour of a single deed,
Which has the imprint of a lover's need
To make the landscape mystic in the vote
He gives the world of beauty, quote
The luminous words among a scrabbled screed,

And saints who'd make of Pegasus a goat.
Here are the flowers, massed among the weed,
Carried by those picadors of greed
Who learn psalms, songs, and apothegms by rote,
And in so doing, do their lessons wrong,
And harvest snow, even from love's even song.
There is a place I know to right the wrong,
There is a place I know I'll find my song.

THE ICE COUNTRY

It is the way I keep on, regardless
Past the ice blocks on the crust of time,
With winter set in, and the sea at my back
Frozen like a long echo

Pledges you had made in warmer climes
Now prove worthless as a translation of hope
They have diminished into raucous laughter
As if there was fun in your self-made joke;

But I keep going, past the time
With the vision of your hands fading,
The beauty of the country, your body
Immobile, presaging this ice age.

It seems we exchanged blood,
Hearts, lights, kidneys, minds,
But not kindness. We had vitriol,
Violence, virulence and pestilence

In the dark green summer. I see
Us imprisoned in a block of ice
Unable to hurt or heal, just prick the skin
With a fleeting irritation, not like a wound.

I keep going past the dead, entombed
Forever in a glacial calm,
Vegetation has long since left the path
There are only stones left, scarring the ice.

THE MERMAID

Could it be called a distance, or a closeness,
This tincture of faith, where our bodies hurt
For each tried arm, or breast, our hopelessness
Sun-starved without real love, sea-girt,

Gulled by the sea's obedience, could our deeds
In the stranded pellet of your wind-off eye
Mark in sea-grass the uncharted needs
Where time believed your oars just drifted by?

Now, rocks are the landscape of my dreams,
Their wimpled arms, their blighted eyes,
Clams opening to my gaze like screams –
How they instruct my usefulness! With lies.

Imperial solitude, past predicating,
My eternal days are without retort,
The shadow of his impossible bones,
Like your battening dreams, a consort.